EDWARD BRUCE

In memory of
Evelyn Hardy
Poet, Author, Voyager

ROGER CHATTERTON-NEWMAN

EDWARD BRUCE

A MEDIEVAL
TRAGEDY

Ian Faulkner Publishing
Cambridge · England

Ian Faulkner Publishing Ltd
Lincoln House
347 Cherry Hinton Road
Cambridge CB1 4DJ

First published May 1992

ISBN 1-85763-009-2

Printed in Great Britain by Billings and Sons Ltd

CONTENTS

LIST OF PLATES

LIST OF MAPS

PREFACE

Edward Bruce, Earl of Carrick and, briefly, King of Ireland, is one of the forgotten actors on the stage of early-fourteenth-century history. Overshadowed by the career of his elder brother, Robert Bruce, King of Scots, Edward is perhaps best remembered for the manner of his death: slain by a 'demented idiot' (at least according to one version) during the Battle of Faughart in Co. Louth on 14th October 1318. Near this spot, sacred to St Brigid and associated with the mythical hero Cuchulain, he had been proclaimed king two brief years earlier. Edward's death recalls that of his ancestor, Brian Boru, High King of Ireland, at Clontarf on Good Friday, 1014. There, however, any similarity between the two men rests. Brian, for a few years, had created a firm central authority within the warring collection of kingdoms and petty principalities that made up Ireland. Edward Bruce attempted to emulate his ancestor, but, unlike Brian, he faced opposition not only from native Irish chieftains but from a strong English administration in Dublin and from one of the most notable Anglo-Irish barons of the period, Richard de Burgh, Earl of Ulster.

Edward's grandfather, Robert Bruce, lord of Annandale, had been a competitor for the throne of Scotland, made vacant by the death of the infant Queen Margaret – known to history as the Maid of Norway – in 1290. A descendant of

King William the Lion, who had ruled Scotland from 1165 to 1214, the elder Bruce was also a substantial landowner in England and, as such, a vassal of the English king, Edward I. When King Edward offered to arbitrate in the selection of a new monarch for Scotland, Bruce supported a suggestion that the country should be partitioned among himself and two other claimants as feudal fiefs, although the idea was turned down by Edward, who selected a kinsman of the Bruces, John Balliol, as Margaret's successor.

Robert Bruce of Annandale died shortly after John Balliol's election, but his claim to the throne passed to his eldest grandson and namesake, the future King of Scots. During the ensuing wars of independence against England and Edward I's hopes for a united Britain, the young Robert was supported by his brother, Edward. Indeed, the brothers were supposedly together in hiding on the island of Rathlin, off the coast of Ireland, in 1306; and it was certainly Edward's recklessness which precipitated the Battle of Bannockburn in 1314 and drove the English from Scotland.

But Edward, Earl of Carrick since his brother's coronation, was ill content with the role of heir presumptive to the throne. John Leland, the antiquary of two centuries later, tells us that he 'demanded to be admitted to an equal share' in Robert's authority, and it is easy to imagine that Robert decided that his brother's energies should be exploited outside Scotland. Whether or not the king opened negotiations with the Celtic princes of Ulster, or whether the King of Aileach, the western division of Ulster, asked for his support, is immaterial. In the spring of 1315, Edward Bruce landed at Olderfleet with an expeditionary force, ostensibly to help the native princes in their struggle with the English administration, in reality to gain a crown of his own.

Ireland was a country torn by internecine strife, notably

in Connacht, the ancient western kingdom whose royal family still claimed the empty title of *Ardri*, or high king, which Brian Boru had once, and briefly, made potent. Rivals for the throne were aided or opposed by magnates such as Richard de Burgh, lord not only of much of Ulster but of great tracts of Connacht; and all paid scant heed to the English administration based in Dublin and headed by the English king's representative, or justiciar.

Edward Bruce's arrival served only to increase the disunity inherent on the Irish political scene. If he entertained hopes of the native Irish flocking to his banner, he was disappointed; and, although for a time he was remarkably fortunate in routing, or out-manoeuvring, opposition, he was never to found a Bruce dynasty in Ulster or any part of Ireland.

Archdeacon Barbour, the eulogist of Robert and Edward Bruce, called the younger brother

> The Erle of Carick, Schyr Eduward,
> That stouter was than a libbard,

but to the Irish annalists he was to be remembered as

> Edward Bruce, the destroyer of all
> Erinn in general.

Doubtless both comments were exaggerated; doubtless both contained more than a grain of truth. Unfortunately, their subject proved too much an interloper, too much a seeker after self-aggrandisement for the Irish who might have supported him. His coronation was an empty gesture, a vain attempt to emulate his brother; and yet down through the intervening centuries it becomes difficult if not wholly to admire then to sympathise with Edward's ambitions. After Bannockburn he was in the shadow of his brother; his

11

attempt to place himself on an equal footing was doomed to failure because he was unable, or unwilling, to recognise his own limitations and those of Ireland. Had he been content to carve himself a kingdom in Ulster, in the manner of the earlier de Lacys and de Burghs, he might have succeeded. As it was, he fell near the place on which he had been crowned; unlike his brother, he was to be buried in soil that had rejected him.

Only one major study of Edward Bruce has been attempted in the past: Olive Armstrong's *Edward Bruce's Invasion of Ireland,* published in 1923; otherwise, apart from brief appearances in the pages of the wider histories of Ireland and Scotland, his name has lain dormant. And while, as ever, he must be regarded in the context of his time, as must his every action, his place in the history of three kingdoms should not be dismissed entirely. Without him, Robert Bruce may not have defeated the army of Edward II at Bannockburn; without him, the merchants of Dublin may never have seized the courage to contain Richard de Burgh, Earl of Ulster; without him, a short but interesting chapter in the annals of Ireland would not have been written.

A student of Edward's life must tread warily through the available source material. The various Irish annals, and Barbour's epic poem, *The Brus,* are prone to wild exaggeration and eulogistic fancy where particular heroes or villains are concerned. Poor translation or editing in later centuries has further complicated the picture, and it must be remembered that many sources were compiled after the events they so vividly describe took place.

Yet it is possible to recreate the events leading up to Edward's birth, and then of his relatively short life. I have referred to the more reliable historians, and a full bibliography will be found in the notes to each chapter.

Acknowledgements

I have received invaluable aid and encouragement from many quarters, and I must thank in particular my friends Betty Craigie and T. J. Barron, the contemporary authority on St Patrick and St Brigid and the leading historian for the district known to Edward Bruce as the principality of Breifne. Thanks are due, too, to the late Dan Nolan, who guided me in the direction of several important sources for reference, to the late John Dermot, whose stories from Ulster history and legend were littered with clues, and to Harold O'Sullivan for confirming the tradition of Bruce's 'grave'. I must also acknowledge the help with illustrations provided so willingly by Alfred Clark and by the Office of Public Works, Dublin, the Irish Tourist Board and the Mary Evans Picture Library.

March 1992   R. C.-N.

Note on Spelling of Irish Proper Names

I must offer an explanation for the use of Irish spelling for personal and family names of the various kings and chieftains. Feidlimidh and Ruaidhridhe O'Conchobhar may be Anglicised as Felim and Rory O'Connor, the phonetical translation of their names; but it would then follow that I should show the name Aedh (ā) as Hugh, which is incorrect. It was a natural error made by the English settlers, unable to pronounce the Gaelic word, but in this case I consider it preferable to leave the names as they would have been known to the compatriots of those who bore them. Thus we have Maelruanaidh Mac Diarmada (mālrōoana mac dēarmida) and not Mulroony Mac Dermot; Toirdhealbhach (turlach), instead of Turlough, and Maoil-Seachlainn (mēlshachlin), rather than the entirely false Malachy.

Conversely, O'Brien came early into use in Ireland in its familiar spelling and I have retained it as such, although preferring Ui Néill (ē nāl) as a dynastic name, rather than the more usual O'Neill, which does not invariably refer to the same clan.

Ardri (awrdrē), *tuatha* (tōoaha) and *rioghdhamhna* (rēghowna) are examples defying all attempts at Anglicisation; while to replace Niall Naoighiallach (nēal nēghealach) with Niall of the Nine Hostages, of the schoolbooks, must be considered cheating.

14

CHAPTER ONE

Insane Counsels, Hopeless Strife

On 22nd February 1300 a 'general invitation came from Rome . . . throughout all Christendom; and in each hundredth year this invitation was wont to be issued, and it was usually called a "year of grace"; and a countless multitude from all the countries in Christendom were wont to go in pilgrimage to Rome at this invitation; and they would obtain forgiveness of all sins through this grace . . . '

So ended, according to the *Annals of Loch Cé*,[1] the thirteenth century, a century in which Christendom in general, and Ireland in particular, had been racked by what a later historian[2] was to describe as 'insane counsels, hopeless strife and pitiless devastation'; a century in which, after eight crusades, the Christians had been driven out of Syria, war raged between church and state in Germany and Italy, civil war twice assailed England and in which, in Ireland, the Hiberno-Norman nobles and the native chieftains vied for territorial supremacy with a ferocity unknown since the coming of the Scandanavian Land Leapers four centuries earlier.

Taken at face value, the Year of Grace, instigated by Pope Boniface VIII, seemed a beacon of hope in a dark world; an opportunity for those who professed the Christian faith to

15

make a new start at the beginning of a new century. Unfortunately, it was an opportunity merely to cast off old sins and start afresh on new, and the personality of the instigator hardly inspired the medieval lords of Europe to reform their own characters, or to emulate those paragons of knightly Christian valour and chivalry portrayed in the contemporary *chansons de geste* or romances.

However much the historian Petrach might eulogise Pope Boniface as 'a man of much learning' and the 'wonder of the world', the pontiff's treatment of his predecessor, Celestine V, whom he forced to abdicate and then imprisoned,[3] and the fact that the Year of Grace was not extended to his personal enemies, illustrates another side of his character. His arguments with Edward I of England and Philip the Fair of France, both of whom objected to papal interference in the affairs of their kingdoms, were pretentious and undignified. He intrigued with rebellious clergy and nobles in Scotland, accepting their overtures and pretending that Scotland had been a papal fief from 'the most ancient times' as a chance to annoy Edward. Later, he was prepared as readily to support Edward in his arguments with Philip.

Apologists for Boniface might claim his intrusions in politics to have been prompted by a misguided righteousness, rather than vulgar ambition; but they none the less epitomised the fatal flaw in the medieval attempt to rule, rather than administer, Christendom. Losing sight of their real mission as successors of St Peter, popes such as Boniface abandoned the salvation of souls to grasp at temporal power. The disgraceful schism that was to rend the Christian world from 1378 until 1429, with a pope in the Vatican acknowledged by the Empire, England and Italy, and another in Avignon supported by Scotland, France, Spain, Cyprus and Sicily, was the climax of this political intrigue.

The arrest of Boniface by French envoys at Anagni in 1303, his rescue by the townsfolk and then his death, supposedly of shock at his treatment, six months later did little for the reputation of the Papacy as far as the nobles and knights of Europe were concerned. Is it surprising that, with so poor an example set at ostensibly so august a level, the first Year of Grace made no impact on the lords, native and foreign, of Ireland? The Irish annalists, usually eager to report the pilgrimage to Rome of a sanguinary prince or peer, have nothing to add to their entries for the year 1300; and while the chance to gain absolution might have proved so popular elsewhere in Europe that the Year of Grace was afterwards reduced in time to a period first of fifty, then of twenty-five, years, its instigation was apparently ignored in the island that once had sent saints and scholars to the courts of Europe.

Insane counsels . . . hopeless strife . . . pitiless devastation is an illuminating, if depressing, description of Irish affairs at the beginning of the fourteenth century. The death of the great king Brian Boru at the weir of Clontarf on Good Friday, 1014, had brought to a close a reign, albeit brief, of diplomacy and intellect remarkable in Irish history. His coronation as *Ardri*, or high king, of Ireland[4] gave reality to a usually meaningless title. His displacement of the Ui Néill clan of Ulster and Meath, which, for six centuries, had claimed hegemony over other kings in Ireland, suggested a turning-point in Irish affairs. The youngest son of an obscure family from north-west Munster, Brian achieved local prominence in 962 when, a youth, he led a band of guerrillas into the moorland and mountains of Clare to harass the Danes of Limerick.

Succeeding to his ancestral throne of Thomond in 976, at the age of thirty-five, he overcame the opposition of native and Danish interests in the southern and eastern kingdoms of Munster and Leinster and, by the end of the tenth century, had established his authority in nearly two-thirds of the island, including the Scandinavian city-state of Dublin. Bloodlessly, but aided by jealousies within the ranks of the Ui Néill, he supplanted Maoil-Seachlainn II of Meath as *Ardri*, and for twelve years halted the native degeneration and internecine strife that had encouraged Scandinavian invasions from 793 onwards.

As Alfred of Wessex, in the last two decades of the ninth century, had brought an era of peace and relative stability to the kingdom across the Irish Sea, with the Danish Guthorm baptised and recognised as King of East Anglia,[5] and the Danelaw, the tract of land between the Scottish borders and a line from the Thames to present-day Liverpool, a definite political entity, so Brian laid the foundations for what might have been a confederation, rather than a fractious welter, of Irish kingdoms. Within sixty years of Alfred's death, Edgar of Wessex was able to call himself King of England, the first to do so with any real conviction; but within weeks of the death of Brian and his able eldest son, Murchadh, Ireland had returned to her old ways of disunity and squabbling. Just as the discord a century before had enabled the Land Leapers to infiltrate the country, so the failure of Irish kings and chieftains of the eleventh and twelfth centuries to learn the lessons of history, and to build upon Brian's foundations, resulted in the next, and greatest, invasion of the island.

> After Maoil-Seachlainn, son of Donal
> Each man ruled his own tribe,
> But no man ruled Erin,

runs an old rhyme. Maoil-Seachlainn regained the high throne after Clontarf and retained it until his death in 1022, but with the exception of Muircheartach Mor, the great-grandson of Brian and *Ardri* from 1086 to 1119, and Toirdhealbhach O'Conchobhar, king of the western state of Connacht for the first half of the twelfth century, no ruler of any calibre appeared to provide Ireland with a leader. The Ui Néill and O'Conchobhar princes alternated in assuming the empty accolade of high king but they failed to unite, either by war or by peaceful methods, their fellow kings.

The events which led to the band of Cambro-Norman mercenaries arriving on Bannow Strand in the spring of 1169 – the elopement of the middle-aged wife of Tiernan O'Ruairc of Breifne with Diarmaid Mac Murchadha of Leinster, Diarmad's expulsion by the self-appointed *Ardri*, Ruaidhridhe O'Conchobhar, and his appeal to Henry II of England – were inevitable. The causes could have been different, or at least a variation on a theme, but the inherent weakness in the superfluity of Irish monarchy, the inclination of the rulers of the principal kingdoms of Ulster, Munster, Leinster and Connacht[6] and of the many *tuaths*, or clannish sub-kingdoms, to regard their neighbours with distrust and envy, would still have brought to Irish shores the Norman empire-builders whose roots were those of the Land Leapers.[7]

Henry II of England, an able king, was determined to make his rule endure, creating an English nation that even the weakest of his successors failed to destroy, and he would tolerate no dissension on his doorstep. Had he died before the invasion of Ireland, it would have come in time, perhaps a century later in the reign of his great-grandson Edward I, who pursued the ideals of a stricter and more defined lordship than these islands had yet known;[8] perhaps later still, in the reign of Edward III, whose ambitions for a greater kingdom began the Hundred Years War with France. Had

only the native Irish kings forgotten their individual grievances, real or imagined, with one another and stood together
to resist the invader, the sequel to the events in Wexford of
1169 might have been different.

As it was, Normans would have crossed the sea with or
without the dubious Bull of Pope Adrian IV, Henry's fellow-
countryman, in which the king was encouraged to 'enter the
island of Ireland, to subject its people to obedience of laws,
to eradicate the seeds of vice, also to make every house pay
the annual tribute of one penny to the Blessed Peter [an
English tribute to the pope, instituted by Ina of the West
Saxons in 725 and paid until suppressed by Henry VIII in
1534] and preserve the rights of the church of that whole land
. . .'[9] Indeed, when Henry II allowed Diarmaid Mac Murchadha to solicit help from the Cambro-Norman barons, the
Bull is supposed to have been thirteen years in existence and
Adrian IV was ten years dead.[10] But neither in 1169, nor
when Henry II himself crossed to Ireland in 1171, was it
mentioned. The Plantagenets, like their Norse forebears,
needed no excuse to extend their dominions, and the attitude
of the Kings of Desmond and Thomond, the principal states
within Munster, and lesser native potentates in recognising
Henry as 'Lord of Ireland' in 1175 served to encourage the
settlement of the country. Little did Henry and his barons
realise that lip-service to an English overlord meant no more
to an Irish king than that given for six centuries to the *Ardri*
of the moment. Henry, marching through Munster and Leinster, had received the pledges of princes, while the Ui Néill
of the north and Ruaidhridhe O'Conchobhar, who called
himself *Ardri*, remained aloof and, initially, unmolested. But
this resistance had characterised the royal progresses of
native overlords throughout history and was no more a
stand against Norman domination than it had been against

the Ui Néill. The giving of pledges and, as security for good behaviour, hostages was a tradition; the time would come to revoke the pledges and perhaps regain the hostages.

The Norman barons replaced the Norse and Danish lords and, like them, became quickly Hibernicised. With Henry again in England and Ruaidhridhe of Connacht maintaining his pretence of high kingship, the old picture of native princes contending for dominion and power with foreigners, of native and foreigner using each other to suit their purpose, was repainted. The years of peace initiated by Brian Boru might never have been, and the only difference between the political situation at the beginning of the fourteenth century and that of the tenth was that the foreigners held the upper hand. Unlike the Land Leapers, settled in their commercial city-states of Dublin, Waterford, Wexford and Limerick, the Normans carved greater estates for themselves, sometimes by marriage, more often by force. While the Vikings had been content, once settled, to be a chain in a Scandinavian trading empire stretching from the Baltic to Byzantium, the heirs of Strongbow were determined to create an empire which could be seen and ridden over, rather than one counted in coin or goods.

The descendants of the Land Leapers had become isolated in everything but trade from their Scandinavian kinsmen by the time Strongbow arrived on Bannow Strand. With no interested king in Norway or Denmark and, since the unification of England in 954, none in Northumbria from whence succour might come, they saw their prosperous city-states crumble as surely as the Irish in the east and midlands saw their kingdoms partitioned among the newcomers.

The spirit of independence or, rather, of tribal instead of national loyalty did not die overnight in Ireland. Indeed, the independence demonstrated by the Cambro-Norman barons, removed by a wide sea and, then, impenetrable forests and bogs from their overlord in England, surely encouraged the Celtic nobility to act as masters of their destiny. The O'Conchobhar kings assumed the meaningless mantle of the Ui Néill in the high kingship: suitably so, as the ancestor of the Ui Néill, Niall Naoighiallach, 'of the Nine Hostages', had launched his march of conquest at the end of the fourth century from Connacht.[11]

It was probably Niall, whose sons Conall, Eanna and Eoghan carved themselves kingdoms in Ulster about AD 400, who attempted to centralise Irish affairs by creating the high kingship, although it was to be centuries before his putative kinsmen in Connacht laid claim to it. The death of Ruaidhridhe O'Conchobhar in 1198 saw the title lapse for ever, but his successors were frequently able and powerful men. The *Annals of Ulster*[12] record the death in 1309 of Aedh Mac Eoghan, King of Connacht, 'one worthy to be high king of Ireland and the one Gaidhel that was . . . greatest and best of figures that came from Brian Boru downwards . . .' Aedh was slain by a 'boorish tanner' at Coill-in-clachain, which may be modern-day Kilclugha in Co. Cavan, and his death is symbolic of the state of affairs among the native aristocracy. Had Connacht been able to forget personal feuds, the kingdom might have been a bastion for the Celtic world against that of the Norman. Aedh's death was commissioned by a kinsman, Aedh Breifnach, who, observed through the dispassionate mists of six centuries, appears alternately as a hero and as a common usurper. He does not seem to have taken the throne of Connacht, but neither did he hand it to the late king's son, the seventeen-year-old Feidlimidh.

Perhaps Aedh Breifnach regarded his own rights to the throne as unquestionable under the law of tanistry, an essential ingredient and often a stumbling-block in Celtic society from the earliest times. It provided for the succession of the eldest male relative of the previous king, rather than that of his eldest son; and if the eldest son were a babe in arms or inexperienced in the defence of his kingdom it could be seen as a wise law. Primogeniture had been recognised slowly in tenth- and eleventh-century England and Europe, except for the Holy Roman Empire where anything but an elective system would have deprived the barons of their power. While the Celts generally abided by the older law, tradition had been dealt a severe blow in Celtic Scotland by Malcolm II, son-in-law of Brian Boru, who reigned from 1005 until his murder at Glamis in 1034. Malcolm extended his power from the Forth to the Tweed, conquering the Anglo-Saxon kingdom of Lothian and finally making Scotland a united country.[13] But he also abrogated the tanistric law in favour of his own descendants, ignoring both the ancient Celtic custom and the Pictish tradition of matriachal descent which had placed several of his predecessors on the throne. Shakespeare's Macbeth, or rather the Macbeth on whom Shakespeare modelled his character, had challenged the new system, for he was of royal blood himself and, through his wife Gruoch, had a claim superior to the family of Malcolm through the Pictish custom.

Thus, Ireland, from where the early colonisers of what became Scotland had taken ship and name, saw not only a change in Europe but a change and resistance in the sister kingdom. It was a change of which both Aedh Breifnach and Feidlimidh tried to take advantage.

The two rivals for Celtic kingship were not the only interested parties in the struggle for supremacy in Connacht. In 1232 the province had been 'given' by Henry III of England to Richard de Burgo, or de Burgh, lord deputy of Ireland for as far as the English writ ran. Like many of the Norman

23

magnates, de Burgh had secured a foothold in Ireland by marrying into the ancient aristocracy, in his case a grand-daughter of Cathal Crovderg, the 'red handed',[14] King of Connacht, who died 'in the habit of a grey friar' in 1224. Cathal had surrendered all, or part, of his kingdom to Henry III, receiving it back as a tenant of the English crown, a part of the feudal machinery the English were determined to impose on Celtic society. Cathal was not alone; the O'Briens of Thomond, heirs of Brian Boru, had made a formal surrender of much of north-west Munster in 1221, receiving it back on payment of an annual rent of one hundred and thirty marks, although the Irish annalists assiduously make no mention of this system of 'surrender and regrant' because, to them, it was an alien and pointless institution. It is left to historians such as Sir Richard Cox and Geoffrey Leland[15] to record it, and there is no reason to suppose that they invented it or acted as apologists for history. None of the old English historians regarded the invasion of Ireland as anything other than an invasion, and while by the time of Cox and Leland the feudal system was extinct, dying with the rest of medieval England in the Wars of the Roses, 'surrender and regrant' was seen as a perfectly necessary part of land tenure. Of course, few if any of the Celtic chieftains took it seriously, but the granting of Connacht to Richard de Burgh after the death of Cathal Crovderg was a different matter. That anything could descend through the female line or by marriage (and de Burgh's heirs would have the blood royal of Connacht in their veins) was to the Celts even more a revolution than primogeniture had been. For while in Scotland the matriarchal system of the Picts had been adopted to secure the succession of early Celtic kings, it was not acknowledged in western Ireland, legends of Queen Maedh notwithstanding.[16] Celtic princes had heard the uproar caused in England less than half a century before the death of Cathal Crovderg by the claims of the Dowager Empress Matilda, daughter of Henry I. The ensuing civil war between that formidable woman and her cousin, King Stephen, had ended in victory for Matilda's son, the future conqueror of Ireland, Henry II. To the Celts, yet to experience Henry and his companions, it would have been blatant usurpation.

Following Cathal's death, 'insane counsels, hopeless strife, pitiless devastation' made up the picture of internal affairs in Connacht. His son, Aedh, claimed the throne, opposed by his cousin, also Aedh, and Toirdhealbhach, sons of Ruaidhridhe who had been the last *Ardri*. The rivalry was fostered by the de Burghs, who had first appeared in Connacht as allies of an opponent of Cathal Crovderg. The arrival on the scene of the Ui Néill of Tir Eoghan resulted in the defeat of Cathal's son and the coronation of Toirdhealbhach. Aedh fled to the English, seeking help from de Burgh and the lord deputy, de Marisco. Aided by Donough O'Brien of Thomond, Aedh's uncle, the English marched into the kingdom and laid it waste. Toirdhealbhach was unable to resist and, deserted by his chieftains, left the throne vacant for Aedh, who now discovered he had unwittingly provided de Burgh with the foothold he needed for taking Connacht as his own.

More bloodshed and dissension followed and, in the end, Aedh accepted an English invitation to a conference at Athlone. There he was murdered and the throne was once more claimed by his cousins, still unable to agree or to form a union against de Burgh. From 1231 until de Burgh's death in 1243 kings were set up and cast down by the men of Connacht or by the English, and it was not until 1256 that the then king, Feidlimidh, another son of Cathal Crovderg, was able to bring a short period of peace to the distracted province. He agreed not to molest any of the English in their possessions, and the integrity of his own dominions was guaranteed by the lord deputy, de la Zouch. The peace was indeed short: in 1260, Feidlimidh was in alliance with the Ui Néill of Tir Eoghan against Walter de Burgh, son of Richard, with the usual consequences. A year or two later the king and de Burgh, who was of course his great-nephew, made peace and, in the language of the annalists, slept together in the same bed 'cheerfully and contentedly'. But they were uneasy bedfellows. Violence was renewed and was to continue up to, and after, the death of Aedh Mac Eoghan in 1309, the de Burghs taking every opportunity to increase their power in the west.

In 1264 the family had extended its interests by the marriage of Walter de Burgh to the heiress of the most powerful Norman in Ireland. She was Maud, daughter of Hugh de Lacy, Earl of Ulster, and brought her husband not only the title but vast estates in the northern kingdom. The original kingdom of Ulster, or Ulaidh, its name probably derived from the founding tribes, had been conquered early in the fourth century[17] by the 'Three Collas', princes of Connacht, the previous inhabitants retreating to what is now County Antrim and Co. Down, where they set up a reduced kingdom bearing the old name of Ulaidh. Then, about AD 400, came the three sons of Niall Naoighiallach, conquering north-west Ulster and establishing the kingdom of Aileach, which was to alternate with Midhe, or Meath, 'the middle', in providing Irish high kings. The throne of Aileach itself alternated between the descendants of Niall's sons, Eoghan and Conall, whose personal territory was known as Tir Eoghan (Tyrone) and Tir Conaill (Tyrconnell), the first spreading out into mid Ulster, the second comprising modern Donegal. By the end of the ninth century Aileach, which

Ireland, showing important places in the story of Edward Bruce

had its capital at the Grianan, a stone fortress north-west of Derry, had subdued what remained of Ulaidh and the King of Aileach appears frequently in the annals as 'King of Ulster'.

But in 1177 the eastern section of the kingdom, the old Ulaidh, fell to John de Courcy, a Norman adventurer from Somerset. Although he never obtained formal title to his conquests from the English king, and never overcame the Ui Néill in Aileach, he was powerful enough to be recorded by the annalists as 'Prince of the Ulaidh' or 'Conqueror of Ulster'; and to consolidate his position he married Affreca, daughter of Godfred, Norse ruler of the Isle of Man, the only southerly inheritance of the Land Leapers to have survived.

De Courcy was by no means a carpetbagger: as a modern historian[18] has written:

He was a noble founder of abbeys, castles and petty towns. His stone castles arose at Carrickfergus, Dundrum and other places; into Down, Inch, Greyabbey and Coleraine he introduced Benedictine and other monks; and along the coast of Antrim and Down and inland to Lough Neagh he enfeoffed his companions, the Hackets, Russels, Savages, Whites and Logans of later times . . .

It was the descendants of those companions who were to resist in vain the landing of Edward Bruce in 1315, and who constituted the first of the many unhappy plantations of Ulster, where the Celtic world withstood them longer than anywhere else in Ireland.

The power of men such as de Courcy was a threat not only to the Ui Néill, who managed to preserve their independence in diminishing form until the sixteenth century, but to the English crown. As the successes of Strongbow attracted the attention of Henry II, who had no intention of allowing his unruly adventurers to become rivals, so did the unlimited power of de Courcy bring upon his head the wrath of Henry's eventual successor, John. Whatever John's faults, he made a serious attempt to resolve the bitterness caused by his father in Ireland. He tried to reduce the power and prestige of de Courcy and his friends, granting smaller tracts of land to new blood, including the families of Barry, Prendergast and Roche. Between 1200 and 1208 he built Dublin Castle as the centre of an administration which would, in theory, legislate impartially for all men, Irish or Norman. He created a state church and, in a move to redress the imbalance of power, confirmed several native princes in their dominions and the Kings of Connacht and Thomond in their kingdoms.

De Courcy was summoned to Dublin by John's deputy, the justiciar Meiler FitzHenry. Refusing to attend, he was besieged in his castle of Dundrum and captured. Exiled to France, where he died in 1219, he saw the kingdom he had created granted, with the title Earl of Ulster, to Hugh de Lacy, whose father had carved himself a feudal state in the centre of Ireland and had married a daughter of the last *Ardri*, Ruaidhridhe O'Conchobhar.

It was de Lacy's daughter and heiress who married Walter de Burgh, bringing Ulster as dowry. The alliance bequeathed to their son, Richard, the greatest feudal estate in Ireland: the north-east and most of the western kingdom of Connacht. It was a powerful inheritance and Richard de Burgh, second Earl of Ulster and lord of Connacht, emerges as the leading magnate on Irish soil. Small wonder that the annalists usually referred to him simply as 'the Earl': everyone knew to whom the title belonged.

Richard de Burgh, known to history as the 'Red Earl' from

the colour of his hair, succeeded his father in 1271. The 'admitted leader of the Anglo-Irish and popular with the Gaels',[19] he enlarged the boundaries of his earldom to the eastern shores of Lough Swilly and, in Connacht, founded the house of Clanricarde (Clan Richard) which, in later years, was to symbolise the adage *Hibernicis ipsis Hiberniores* and supersede the O'Conchobhar princes in feuding and rivalry. He also bequeathed his heirs more than a drop of royal Celtic blood: through his grandmother he was descended from Cathal Crovderg, through his mother from the last *Ardri*, Ruaidhridhe. In Norman eyes the de Burghs were no less fitted to rule Connacht as the O'Conchobhar.

Richard de Burgh's power far outshone that of John de Courcy. He made and unmade kings in Connacht but never took the throne for himself, and he maintained friendly relations with one or other of the rival royal factions, suggesting how much he relied on the Celts to augment his forces. And as the men of Connacht had little love for the Ui Néill, they were used to good effect in extending de Burgh's influence in the north. In 1286 he marched into Tir Eoghan and deposed the king Domhnall Ui Néill, afterwards King of Aileach, replacing him with Niall Culanach Ui Néill, whom Domhnall's supporters promptly slew. He fought a long and bitter feud with the FitzGeralds, lords of Naas and Offaly in the eastern kingdom of Leinster, who had aided the first Richard de Burgh in his invasion of Connacht.

In 1294 the earl was captured by the FitzGeralds and released only after the intervention of the justiciar, Sir John de Wogan. A conscientious administrator, Sir John was placed in an embarrassing position over the earl: de Burgh was married to a cousin of Queen Eleanor, much lamented wife of Edward I of England, and had the ear of the king, joining him in the invasion of Scotland in 1296, when he

30

received from the treasury £5,014 13s. 4d. as expenses. His capture by the FitzGeralds caused the 'disturbance of all Ireland' according to the usually laconic *Annals of Ulster*.

There were similar disturbances when de Burgh was in Scotland, Irishmen and lesser 'foreigners' taking the opportunity to attempt to change the balance of power in Connacht and Ulster.

Certainly, power in Connacht was in the balance during the first decade of the fourteenth century. The murder of Aedh Mac Eoghan in 1309 was followed a year later by the death of his supplanter, Aedh Breifnach. The *Annals of Loch Cé* record his death as a tragedy for Ireland in general (as the *Annals of Ulster* had recorded that of his victim), for Aedh Breifnach was 'the best qualified to be king that was in Erinn in his own time, if it had pleased God to allow it'. His death, like that of Aedh Mac Eoghan, was caused by conspiracy and the connivance of the de Burghs. He was slain by Mac Quillan, leader of his *buannadha*, or militia, for the maintenance of which Irish chieftains had for centuries extracted *bonaght* or *buanaght* from their subjects. But if the Red Earl imagined he had disposed of a troublesome Celt he was mistaken: at once Feidlimidh, young son of Aedh Mac Eoghan and a direct descendant of Cathal Crovderg, was proclaimed King of Connacht by his foster-father, Maelruanaidh Mac Diarmada, chieftain of Moylurg in Roscommon, whose descendants were responsible for compiling the *Annals of Loch Cé*. Fosterage, a practice common among the Irish chieftains,[20] inspired greater loyalty than did blood relationship, and Mac Diarmada knew his duty, even if it did deprive him for a time of his hereditary possessions.

Observing 'his foster-son ignored regarding his inheritance, and feeling strongly that the Foreigners were restricting his power' – an understatement by the *Annals of Loch Cé*

31

– Mac Diarmada decided to 'elevate his foster-son over all
... and forcibly to make him king, without much delay. And
he took him with him upon Carn-Fraich-mhic-Fidhaigh [the
inauguration place of the kings of Connacht near modern-
day Tulsk, three miles south-east of Rathcroghan, Co. Ros-
common] and inaugurated him on the carn according to the
practice of the saints ... and in the most regal, most illustrious, and fullest manner that any man of his own family
had been inaugurated ... down to that day ...'[21] After the
young king had 'espoused the province of Connacht, moreover, his guardian administered to him that night in accord-
ance with the tradition of the old men, and the old books;
and this was the most regal, and most illustrious, wedding
feast of a king that had ever been made for a King of Connacht until that day ...', the wedding feast alluding to the
old Celtic custom that held a king must be married to his
kingdom.

Alas, Feidlimidh's reign was to be brief and troubled,
much of it spent as a wanderer in his own lands. Despite the
powerful imagination of the annalists, there was to be no
resurgence of an independent Celtic monarchy in Connacht.
Had other members of the royal house accepted Feidlimidh's inauguration, they might have emulated, with some
degree of success, the Ui Néill in Aileach who, while paying
occasional homage to the Red Earl, maintained their authority until 1540. As it was, Feidlimidh's right to the throne
was challenged immediately by his kinsman, Ruaidhridhe,
brother of Aedh Breifnach, who also assumed the title of
king.

The administrative machine set up by King John, and later
remodelled by Edward I, proved ineffective in maintaining
English law in Ireland. Legislation might be passed forbid-

ding the colonists to wear their hair in Celtic fashion – the 'glib' across the forehead or the 'collun' of flowing locks; every freeholder of twenty ploughlands might be ordered to keep armour and horse for state service, and representative parliaments, so called, might be summoned to enact such legislation. But it was ignored by the colonists as it was by the natives; and while successive justiciars, representatives of the English king, attempted to impose orderly English offialdom on both factions, the only real law was that of the sword. *Lamh laidir aboo*, 'the strong hand to victory', battle-cry of the O'Briens of Thomond, could well have been adopted as a motto by diverse and conflicting interests in the Year of Grace, 1300.

Another Celtic adage, *Tir mharbh tir gan tighearna*, 'a land without a lord is a dead land', was equally apposite, in that there was no overlord in the island. Edward I, greatest of the English kings since Henry II, was preoccupied with wars in Wales, France and, since the end of the thirteenth century, Scotland. De Wogan and other justiciars were told to make Ireland a self-sufficient unit of Edward's British dominions, but they were hardly given the necessary resources, financial or military. While de Wogan could provide Edward with levies for his wars elsewhere, and while men like de Burgh did not cavil about accompanying him, the king – Edward *Mor*, the great, as the annalists called him – could not concern himself with internal rivalries and feuds.

In 1307 Edward died. Seven years later, on Midsummer Day, a mighty English army was defeated at Bannockburn, near Stirling, in Scotland. The *Annals of Clonmacnoise* record laconically: 'There was a battle fought by Robert Bruce, King of Scotland, against the Englishmen, where the said Robert in defence of his Kingdome killed an infinite number of earls, knights and nobles of England, with a great slaughter of theire Inferiours . . .' The new King of England and lord of Ireland, luckless Edward II, fled southwards, his army overthrown by a man who was as much a Norman baron as the Red Earl. Curiously, Robert Bruce was to provide incentive sufficient for a handful of Celtic chieftains to make a stand against the English administration in Ireland. His brother, Edward, was to be welcomed in Larne Bay by Domhnall Ui Néill of Aileach and was to prove as great a source of native aspiration as the Red Earl himself.

CHAPTER TWO

Competing for a Crown

Edward Bruce, future King of Ireland, has been eclipsed in history by the exploits, real or apocryphal, of his elder brother, Robert, King of Scotland. Yet neither might have achieved a place in history had it not been for an accident on the night of 19th March 1286.[1] Alexander III, King of Scots, had that day attended a council meeting in Edinburgh Castle: his wife of a year, the Frenchwoman Yolande of Dreux, was awaiting him at Kinghorn, on the north side of the Firth of Forth and, despite the stormy night and attempts by his courtiers to dissuade him, the king set out to join her.

After a difficult crossing of the Forth by ferry, Alexander was nearing his destination when his horse stumbled on the cliff edge: the king fell to his death on the rocks below, and

> Scotland lamented him full sore,
> For under him all his people were
> In honour, quiet and in peace.
> Therefore called Peaceable King he was.[2]

It was to be a generation before a semblance of peace came again to the northern kingdom. Alexander's death brought to an end the rule of a dynasty which, in tradition at least, had its origins in Fearghus mac Earca, a prince of the north-eastern Irish kingdom of Dal Riada, comprising much of modern County Antrim, who in the late fifth century impressed his sovereignty on what today is Argyll.[3] His descendants, putative or proven, ruled there for over three centuries, warring with their Pictish neighbours, the aboriginal inhabitants, and providing a haven for monkish evangelists during the heyday of ecclesiastical peregrinations in the sixth and seventh centuries. Among them was Colum Cille, or Columba, who founded the monastery of Iona in 563.

In time, however, the marauding longboats of the Norsemen (preceded, according to the *Anglo-Saxon Chronicle*, by 'terrible portents', of which 'exceptional flashes of lightning and fiery dragons' were the more dramatic) broke the link between Irish Dal Riada and its colony across the sea. The first became an integral part of Ulaidh, or Ulster, the second the embryo kingdom of Alba which was to grow into Scotland[4] – although it was to take the Kings of Alba until 1018 to unite the different interests in north Britain into one realm.

In 843 Cinaeth II, surnamed mac Alpin, united the Scots, as the people of Alba were known, and the Picts by marriage and massacre;[5] and at the beginning of the eleventh century his descendant Malcolm II overcame the Anglo-Saxon rulers of Lothian, bringing Edinburgh (*Edwinsburgh*) into Scottish hands. So, too, he gained power over the Britons of Strathclyde, or Cumbria, extending the boundaries of his kingdom from the Forth to the Tweed.

Although the Scottish monarchy was, like its neighbours in Ireland, elective rather than hereditary, the throne was a strong symbol of unity; the dynasty secure. Four years after Brian Boru's hopes for a strong centralised Irish monarchy were dashed at Clontarf, his son-in-law, Malcolm II, had partly by inheritance, partly by military success, gained a position in Scotland which for centuries the most powerful of the Ui Néill had failed to achieve in Ireland. Despite outside interference, the Scottish monarchy survived and its eventual representative was to unite the crowns of Scotland and England in 1603.

Scotland, in the years when a young prince of Thomond was launching his meteoric career in Ireland, and when the heirs of Alfred of Wessex were expelling the Norsemen from York, had an advantage over its neighbours. The fragmented nature of the Irish and English polity had prevented the growth of definite nationhood and had left both countries open to attack from Scandinavian adventurers. In Ireland, as we have seen, the multiplicity of *tuaths* grouped loosely within the various kingdoms provided a breeding-ground for internecine strife, of which the Norsemen took advantage. Only the nature of the island, with impenetrable forest and bogs covering much of the south and midlands until as late as the seventeenth century,[6] and occasional resistance from men such as Brian Boru, prevented the newcomers overrunning it completely. In England, where the title of *bretwalda*, chief among the rulers of the heptarchy of kingdoms, was more often than not as meaningless as that of *Ardri*, local or provincial pride was equally damaging to resistance. Men of Wessex or Mercia, like men of Munster or Connacht, did not regard themselves as citizens of a nation other than Wessex or Mercia. The Danish occupation of the once-powerful realm of Northumbria (of which Lothian had once been part) and the capture of York in 867 had been accomplished because of Northumbrian civil disorder.[7]

The greatest Saxon king of his time, Offa of Mercia, had died in 796 on the eve of the Norse invasions; the good King Eanred of Northumbria died in 840, after an unprecedented reign of thirty-two years, and the birth of Alfred was nine years in the future. In course of time, Alfred's victories saved southern England and prevented, for the moment, Danish expansion; but he did not break the power of the Danelaw, that area north of a line from the Thames to modern Liverpool. Indeed, the Treaty of Wedmore in 878 between Alfred and Guthorm recognised the partition of England; and, the high calibre of Alfred's immediate heirs and the end of Danish Northumbria notwithstanding, it was a Dane, the great Cnut, who brought England real peace and a code of law enshrining justice and the individual rights of his subjects.

But in Scotland, or Alba, union of native interests had started in the middle of the ninth century, and while the Western Isles were colonised by Norsemen and were ceded to Scotland only in 1264, the house of Alpin held the throne without opposition.

Inevitably, feuds arose within the royal house itself. The action of Malcolm II, king from 1005 until 1035, in abrogating the right of elective succession to his own descendants, excluding the heirs of Cinaeth III whom he had supplanted, was successful because the immediate heirs of Cinaeth were women. Of course, the Pictish system of monarchy had been matrilineal and Cinaeth mac Alpin adapted that system when he became ruler of the Picts. Between the death of mac Alpin in 859 and the accession of Malcolm II, only one king, Eocha (878–89) had been elected because the blood royal ran in his mother's veins: but Malcolm's wife, or wives, bore him three daughters. And while two of them were to be mothers of kings – Duncan I and Macbeth – the family of Cinaeth III could argue that, as Malcolm's abrogation had not resulted in sons as heirs, their own line had a senior claim to the throne on his death.

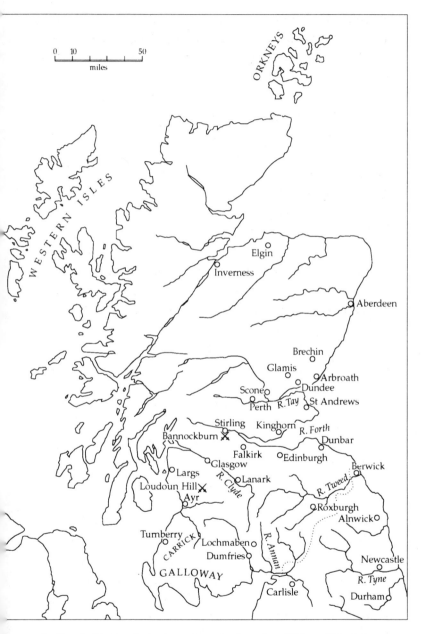

Scotland, showing important places in the story of Edward Bruce

Malcolm II was determined to found a real dynasty in Scotland. As the son-in-law of Brian Boru he could hardly fail to be influenced by what was happening in Ireland, particularly the grooming of Brian's eldest son, Murchadh, as heir, the presence of older princes of Thomond notwithstanding. That Brian, on becoming *Ardri*, had rejected tradition by not resigning his own kingdom of Munster, suggested that the high kingship was to remain in his descendants' keeping,[8] also Munster and Thomond. It suggested, too, that in this instance tanistric law would be set aside.

The death of Brian and Murchadh on the same day returned Ireland to a period of fragmented dissension; while in England any successes of Alfred and, later, Edgar (959–75) were similarly negated for the lack of a strong king. The weak Ethelred II, surnamed the Redeless, proved a fine target for new Danish adventurers, and, in 1013, England became a Danish colony through the efforts of Svein Forkbeard, father of Cnut.

If Scotland was to be spared a repetition of the tragedies of England and Ireland, the succession could hardly be left to chance and the hope that the *tanaiste*, or elected heir, of the moment would prove capable of holding that which Malcolm had won. There was no guarantee that primogeniture was an improvement on the old system, but possibly Malcolm, like his father-in-law, had faith in the princes of his own loins.

By the time of Malcolm's death, the recognised heir was Duncan, son of his eldest daughter. When still a boy, Duncan had been made King of Strathclyde by his grandfather – Brian, it should be noted, created no subsidiary titles – following a custom adopted from the Saxons.[9] About the same time, Malcolm gave the territories of Caithness and Sutherland to another grandson, Thorfinn, although the point of the exercise is vague in that those lands were ruled not by Malcolm but by Thorfinn's paternal Norse relations.

Thorfinn's father was Sigurd, Earl of the Orkneys, who died fighting Brian Boru (who, by the convoluted dynastic alliances of the day, was also his grandfather-in-law) and represented the only dynastic alliance made by Malcolm through his daughters. While Brian married his daughters into strategic kingdoms – Scotland, Dublin and, his old rival for the throne of Munster, Desmond – Malcolm found Scottish noblemen for his eldest and youngest daughters. Of course, after 1018, the Orkneys were outside Malcolm's jurisdiction, but the marriage had taken place at least four years earlier, when Lothian and Strathclyde were still to be conquered.

Malcolm's generosity to his grandsons, and his apparent belief in their ability, backfired after his death, an event which occurred at Glamis and was probably assassination, although Shakespeare translated place and cause to the next reign. Duncan became King of Scots; but Thorfinn, who, because of his empty childhood title, was 'precocious in growing up immediately to full manhood',[10] considered he had an equal right to the throne. When barely thirteen, he laid claim to his father's Orcadian earldom, then divided between his elder half-brothers, Somerled, Brusi and Einar Ragmund.[11] In 1018 he was assigned the share of the short-lived Somerled and, two years later, claimed that of Einar, launching twenty years of civil war in which the Kings of Norway, nominal overlords of the Orkneys, interfered, and which left Thorfinn at times the master, at others a pensioner of the Norse court.[12]

Problems over succession in the Orkneys posed no great

threat to the King of Scots until 1037, when, in the company of Ragnvald II of Norway, Thorfinn invaded the mainland and, two years later, defeated his cousin Duncan at the Battle of Torfness. Then entered on the Scottish stage the third of Malcolm's grandsons.

This was Macbeth, son of the *mormar*, or great steward, of Moray and in 1040 a commander in Duncan's army. Whether Macbeth murdered Duncan in the retreat from Torfness (tradition, not Shakespeare, says that the crime was committed at Bothnagowan, now Pitgaveny, near Elgin) or whether Duncan died of wounds received during the battle is immaterial. Macbeth became King of Scotland, without a prophecy told on a blasted heath, and under tanistric law had every right so to do, being the senior descendant of Malcolm after Duncan's death. Duncan's sons, the young Malcolm and Donald *Ban*, or white, probably referring to his fair hair, fled to Northumbria. There they took refuge with the family of their uncle Maldred, a brother of Duncan who had married a daughter of the Danish-Saxon Earl of Northumbria. Later, Malcolm was to go south to the court of Edward the Confessor, so beginning the long and unfortunate English connection. Donald *Ban* may have sought refuge with his relatives in Ireland.

For the next seventeen years Macbeth ruled wisely and well.[13] In 1050 he went on pilgrimage to Rome, which would suggest that Scotland was settled and unlikely to break into revolt during the monarch's necessarily lengthy absence. One imagines that Macbeth had the support of many chieftains who had opposed Malcolm's interference with the tanistric principle; and now it seemed that this high-handed abrogation of an ancient law would be revoked. Macbeth's heir was his stepson, Lulach, through his mother, Gruoch – Shakespeare's over-maligned 'Lady Macbeth' – a great-grandson of the senior line of Cinaeth III, and thus entitled to the throne by matrilineal descent.

In 1054 Duncan's son Malcolm, surnamed *Ceann Mor* or 'big head', referring presumably to cranium size, rather than ego, invaded Scotland with his kinsman, Siward of Northumbria. Macbeth was defeated at Scone and the regions of Lothian and Strathclyde (or Cumbria as it was then generally known) fell to Malcolm. The war continued until 1057, when Macbeth was killed at Lumphanan in Aberdeenshire, history being silent on whether or not a moving wood was involved. But Malcolm was not yet king of all Scotland: Lulach was crowned at Scone in August of the same year and held out for seven months until he was killed by Malcolm at Essie, Strathbogie, on St Patrick's Day, 1058. He was known as Lulach the Simple but his death was accomplished 'by stratagem',[14] which suggests he was no easy victim to ensnare.

The accession of Malcolm *Ceann Mor* as Malcolm III returned the throne to the heirs of Malcolm II, with whom it remained until the death of Alexander III at Kinghorn in 1286. And while a modification of the tanistric law was indeed to apply for years to come, remoter branches of the family were not regarded as *rioghdhamhna*, or blood royal.

The death of Macbeth saw the beginning of the end of a purely Celtic monarchy in Scotland, for while the first wife of Malcolm III was probably a daughter of his half-Scottish cousin Thorfinn,[15] his second was Margaret of England, St Margaret to her adopted subjects, sister of the exiled English pretender Edgar *Atheling*. They were married in 1069, three years after Margaret and her family sought refuge in Scotland from the invading William of Normandy. Margaret was a cosmopolitan, compared with her husband's family. She had been brought up at the court of Hungary – indeed, had been born there – to escape the attentions of Earl Godwin of Wessex, and was well versed in the flowering culture of early medieval Europe. She was a striking contrast to previous Scottish queen consorts and did much to wean Scotland from its Celtic ways, not least assimilating the church with the rest of Christendom.

While it should be stressed that the so-called Celtic church differed only from its Roman parent on localised points, such as the due commencement of Easter, and was never a church separate from, or antagonistic to, Rome, it had become isolated in the long years when Norsemen prevented evangelists from crossing the seas. In Ireland, the situation was similar, but sadly there was no St Margaret on hand: had there been, England might never have fallen back on a spurious Papal Bull as an excuse for invasion.

Celtic tradition took some time to die. After Malcolm III was killed at Alnwick, during an invasion of Northumbria in 1093, the throne was claimed by his brother, Donald *Ban*, then aged about sixty and described by a contemporary as an 'incorrigible old Celt'.[16] Malcolm's sons followed the earlier footsteps of their father and fled to England, where William Rufus saw them as an opportunity to extend his rule north of the border.

By 1097 Malcolm's heir, Edgar, had won the throne with the help of an English army, having acknowledged William Rufus as his feudal overlord. Such allegiance meant no more to Edgar, or to the Scots, than did the homage paid to an Irish *Ardri*. But the Scots did not understand the machinations of the feudal system, and their acknowledgement of the English king as overlord, the price paid to regain a throne, sowed dragons' teeth for the future.

From the time of Edgar primogeniture finally banished the Celtic elective system for the throne, and from his time, too, Scottish kings and princes looked towards England for their brides. Alexander I, Edgar's successor, married the illegitimate daughter of Henry I of England, while Henry himself married Alexander's sister, Matilda, known to her subjects as 'Good Queen Maud'. Gradually, Scotland divided into the old and the new world, the Highlands retaining their tribal flavour, the Lowlands and borders reflecting English customs and interests, invoking a Highland contempt not yet dead.

During the reign of Alexander I, the Lowlands were controlled by his youngest brother, David, whose marriage to the daughter of another Northumbrian magnate, Waltheof, brought him the English earldom of Huntingdon – for which he duly paid homage at Westminster. David had already been made King of Cumbria and by the time he came to the Scottish throne in 1124 he had surrounded himself with Anglo-Norman barons seeking brides and land (which were synonymous) in his kingdom.

David supported his niece, the Dowager Empress Matilda, during her quarrels with Stephen of England for the crown. He made frequent incursions into England, officially as Earl of Huntingdon and a loyal vassal of Matilda; doubtless, too, with that inherent Celtic love of fighting which the Anglicisation of the royal house failed to eradicate completely. In 1138 he ravaged Northumbria and Yorkshire, technically on Matilda's behalf, and found himself opposed by the aged and crippled Archbishop of York, Thurstan, who was Stephen's deputy in the north. Ill as he was, Thurstan rallied the English barons at York and at Cowton Moor,[17] three miles above Northallerton, soundly defeated the Scots in an engagement that has become known as the Battle of the Standard because of the ship's mast, mounted on a wagon, to which was attached a consecrated wafer and the arms of

SS Peter of York, Wilfrid of Ripon, John of Beverley and Cuthbert of Durham. Among the barons on the English side the names of Bruce and Balliol should be noted.

David's grandson, William the Lion, who came to the throne in 1165, also invaded England. His predecessor, Malcolm IV, the Maiden, so called from his youthful appearance, had been confirmed in his earldom of Huntingdon by Henry II of England but in return for the disputed Cumbrian lands. Now, William determined to recover what for so long had been part of Scotland; unfortunately, on 13th July 1174, he fell into the hands of the English near Alnwick Castle – the scene, eighty years before, of the death of Malcolm III – and was taken captive to Normandy. There, by the Treaty of Falaise, he agreed to perform homage for his kingdom, in return for liberation.

It was only the pressing need of that other 'lion', Richard I of England, for funds for his crusades that saw the miserable treaty revoked in return for 10,000 marks. But the claims over Scotland were renewed in 1250 by Richard's nephew, Henry III: William the Lion's grandson, Alexander III, destined to be the last of the old Scottish royal house, came to the throne as a child and Henry immediately appealed to Pope Innocent IV for a declaration that the child was a liege subject of the English crown. The pope, however, reprimanded Henry:

We will not grant anything to any man which we hold to be prejudicial to the dignity of a king . . . to grant such a thing to anyone in another kingdom is altogether unheard of . . .

which was an interesting comment in the light of an earlier pope's brief to an earlier Henry of England on subjecting 'people to obedience of laws' in Ireland. Even if the validity of the Irish Bull is in question, it is also in striking contrast to Innocent's interference in continental politics and his battle for supremacy with the German emperor, Frederick.

Initially, Henry gained a foothold in Scotland without papal assistance: in 1251 or 1252 he married his elder daughter, Margaret, to Alexander, whom he also knighted. Alexander, though young, was no innocent. He paid homage to his father-in-law for his English lands but excused himself for so doing for Scotland. The Scottish court supported this move and Henry turned once more to Pope Innocent, now in need of funds to maintain his feud with the emperor.

Henry, whose piety gained fanatical heights, allowed the pope to tax the English clergy without mercy[18] and offered no objection to the pope's promise to his Roman subjects of the next three hundred benefices to fall vacant in England. By 1254 Innocent had revised his opinions on the dignity of kingship and granted Henry a twentieth of the ecclesiastical revenues of Scotland.

But Innocent's demands on England shortly aroused anti-papal feeling, to culminate three centuries later in the Reformation. More immediately, it brought civil war and the rise of the great Simon de Montfort; and within four years Henry was powerless to press his claims on Scotland. At the same time a Scottish equivalent of de Montfort, Walter Comyn, Earl of Menteith, appeared on the scene: Henry recognised Alexander's court and the young king, aged now about twenty, settled down to rule his country without fear of intervention from his neighbour.

Yet, while the Scots showed an unusual ability to recognise the benefits of belonging to a nation, Alexander faced another major threat. In 1263 Haakon IV of Norway led an expedition, first to the Orkneys, receiving the homage of his nominal vassal, Earl Magnus III, and then along the western coast to the Firth of Clyde and on towards Ayrshire. At

Largs, in Cunningham, the invaders prepared to land but, as three centuries later England was to be saved by the elements from the Spanish Armada, so now a tempest conveniently, or providentially, arose to help Scotland. Haakon's fleet, said by the fourteenth-century chronicler, Fordun, to number one hundred and sixty longboats, was scattered. The Norsemen who disembarked were slaughtered or routed by the Scots and Haakon retreated to the Orkneys, where he died on 16th October of the same year.

The Western Isles were transferred to the Scottish crown by the Treaty of Perth and thus, nearly two and a half centuries after Malcolm II subdued Lothian and Strathclyde, his descendant became master of virtually the last corner of Scotland owing allegiance to a foreign power. The Orkneys remained in the nominal possession of Norway until 1469, when they were ceded to Scotland as the dowry of Margaret of Norway, bride of James III.[19]

The armada of 1263 was the last attempt by the Norsemen to resurrect their sea-powered empire. It was outdated: the death-knell of the Vikings had sounded in 1066, a few weeks before the Battle of Hastings, when Harald Sigurdsson of Norway fell at Stamford Bridge challenging the throne of Harold Godwinson of Wessex. At this period in history it is too easy to be a partisan of the 'last of the Saxon kings' (who was, in any case, half Danish, his mother being a niece of Cnut) and easy to forget that the Norwegian monarch's claim was seen by many people at the time as legitimate.

The last of the old Saxon royal line, Ethelred the Redeless and his son, Edward the Confessor, had proved themselves unsuited to high office: the first through cowardice, the second through ill-timed piety. But between Ethelred and Edward had come Cnut, under whom England prospered and, in time, rose above its ignominious position as a Scan-

dinavian colony. The Saxons who fought for Harald Sigurdsson at Stamford Bridge saw the Norwegian as a successor to
Cnut, who had ruled both Denmark and Norway, and they
were no less loyal than those of their countrymen who fell
beneath the raven banner at Hastings.

From 1263 Alexander could rule Scotland wisely and well.
The year of Haakon's defeat saw the birth of his son, also
Alexander, known as the Prince of Scotland, in whom the
future of the dynasty seemed secure. With English interference minimal and Scandinavian threats abated – in 1281
Alexander was to marry his daughter to Erik II of Norway
as a further token of peace – Scottish prosperity was assured.
In the late 1270s another son was born to the king and queen,
and christened David; but then the fate that follows thrones
stepped in. Queen Margaret died, mourned by the nation, in
1275, followed seven years later by the infant David. In 1283
the Prince of Scotland died, without issue, and the sole heir
to the throne was his sister, wife of the King of Norway. She
joined her mother and brothers a year later, leaving an infant
daughter as heir presumptive to Scotland.

In 1285 King Alexander married again, this time to
Yolande of Dreux, but according to the chroniclers the wedding feast was marred by the appearance of a phantom, said
by some to be Death himself. Less than five months later
Alexander fell to his death; Yolande was expecting no children.

The little Maid of Norway, as she is known to history, was
acknowledged as Queen Margaret of Scotland, but she never
saw her kingdom. The following dignitaries were appointed
regents until Margaret was considered old enough to travel
from Norway: William Fraser, Bishop of St Andrews; Duncan, Earl of Fife, who had the hereditary right to crown the
new monarch; Robert Wishart, Bishop of Glasgow; James,

steward of the realm; and John Comyn of Badenoch. By 1289 they were at odds with each other, and Erik of Norway, fearful for his daughter's realm, sought the help of Edward I of England in settling the dispute.

By the Treaty of Brigham, the following year, Margaret was engaged to the Prince of Wales, afterwards the hapless Edward II; a peaceful union of the two kingdoms seemed inevitable and Margaret set sail to claim her inheritance and her groom. Alas, she died in the Orkneys, and her body was not even to rest in Scottish soil. Erik, wishing to ensure that the story of her death was true, had the body returned to Norway. Thus later folk-tales of the little queen being kidnapped can be confidently dismissed.

The throne was vacant, no immediate heir obvious. The regents, from whose ranks Duncan of Fife had disappeared, carried on the government of Scotland to the best of their abilities, fearful of 'a great war and a general slaughter of men'.[20] On 10th May 1291 Edward of England arrived at Northam, Northumbria, announcing that he came out of pity and 'as the superior and lord paramount of the kingdom of Scotland', the claim surrendered by Richard I in return for 10,000 marks. Edward did not claim the throne but offered to help the Scots in the selection of a new king, one doubtless who could help Edward achieve his ambition of a single law for Britain, with himself the overlord of an island empire. The regents, realising that civil war or invasion was the alternative to the king's offer, accepted it, perhaps not unwilling to pass the task of selecting their new king to an outsider. And it was no easy task: there were no fewer than thirteen claimants, a mixed bag of Anglo-Scottish noblemen, petty princes and two foreign monarchs.

Heading the list was Florence V, Count of Holland, great-grandson of Ada, eldest daughter of David I's only son, Henry. He ruled Holland, since the tenth century a tributary state of the Holy Roman Empire, as a vassal. The Scottish throne was a valuable prize.

Next came Patrick Dunbar, eighth Earl of Dunbar and the great-grandson of another Ada, this one the second daughter of William the Lion. Dunbar was more English noble than Scotsman; he was descended in the male line from the Saxon rulers of Northumbria and his title was an English creation. He had also been made Earl of March, an honour awarded at the discretion of English kings.

William Vesci, another Englishman, was grandson of William the Lion's third daughter, Margaret; and fourth was William Ros, great-grandson of Margaret's eldest sister, Isabella. Fifth was Robert Pinkney, descended from the youngest sister of William the Lion; and sixth Nicholas Soules, second cousin of the Maid of Norway and the only descendant of Alexander II to appear.

The seventh claimant was Patrick Galithy, grandson of William the Lion, but probably illegitimate; the eighth, Roger Mandeville, a Norman and the great-great-grandson through two female lines of William the Lion's youngest daughter, Aufrica. But, as with the other descendants of William the Lion, neither Galithy nor Mandeville appears to have been taken seriously.

The ninth claimant was John Comyn of Badenoch, one of the regents of Scotland, and arguably the only contender to have first-hand experience of Scottish affairs. But his claim was based on blood royal diluted through six generations, his nearest ancestor to have held the throne being that 'incorrigible old Celt' Donald *Ban*, deposed in 1097. Comyn was descended from Donald's daughter, Bethoc, but he was married to the sister of another claimant, John Balliol, whose

51

own claim, and that of the next two claimants, was based on descent from David of Huntingdon, youngest brother of William the Lion.

It was these three – Balliol, grandson of the eldest of David's daughters; John Hastings, Lord Abergavenny, grandson of the third daughter; and Robert de Bruce, lord of Annandale, son of the second daughter and also descended from William the Lion – around whom the contest revolved in earnest. A claim by Erik of Norway, as representative of his daughter, was discounted.

Balliol, Hastings and Bruce had a major advantage over the other contestants: all three were powerful magnates with considerable estates in Scotland and were already liege men of the English king.

Indeed, so much an Englishman was Hastings that he suggested to King Edward that Scotland should be partitioned among the three as feudal fiefs, the old names of Alba, Lothian and Strathclyde being revived for the purpose. Yet, however much it might have been in Edward's interest to recreate the ancient territories, fragmentation was alien to his hopes for an eventual single state of Britain.

Tripartition was also supported by Bruce, who, at the age of eighty-one, could hardly be considered long for this world. He had once been influential on both sides of the border, serving Henry III of England as Chief Justice of the King's Bench from 1249 to 1250 and fighting for him at the Battle of Lewes against Simon de Montfort in 1264.

More interestingly, he claimed to have been appointed heir presumptive to Alexander II in 1238, before the birth of the future Alexander III, but this carried no weight in 1291. Although Bruce negotiated an agreement for 'mutual defence' with Florence of Holland in 1292, he was powerless to do more than register a protest against Edward's eventual selection.

The choice was John Balliol, the decision turning on whether, as a modern historian has pointed out,[21] the 'custom of Scotland' gave the son of a younger daughter a better right than the grandson of an elder; and, when the Scottish auditors failed to agree, the English judges made the choice for them. A lengthy debate produced an argument, as obviously it would, in favour of English usage, whereby the elder line must be extinguished before succession passes to the junior. On such a point civil war between Stephen and Matilda had divided England, with the senior line at length gaining the throne. And, as great-grandson of the victor, Edward I held firmly to the principle that won the Plantaganets the crown. Perhaps conveniently ignored was the fact that when his ancestor, Henry II, was made heir to Stephen the only other claimant was Stephen's imbecile son.

So John Balliol – 'Toom Tabard', or empty coat, as he was shortly to be known by his subjects – was to be king. But Bruce carefully avoided recognising his rival by making over his own rights to his son. He, in turn, made over his Scottish estates to his own eighteen-year-old son, also Robert, later to become the most celebrated king in Scottish history. The other claimants apparently accepted Balliol's election.

On 17th November 1292 the first interregnum in the Scottish monarchy came to an end. John Balliol was crowned at Scone on a stone which tradition maintained had once served a similar purpose at Tara in Ireland.[22] Within weeks he found himself a figurehead, ignored or insulted by his people. 'A simple creature, who opened not his mouth, fearing the frenzied wildness of his people, lest they should starve him or shut him up in prison' is a contemporary description of King John of Scotland. 'English courts offered

EDWARD BRUCE

better justice than could be obtained in Scotland'[23] is an
illuminating observation, yet one wonders whether John
was so simple a man, or as frightened of the Scots, as has
been suggested. Why did he claim the throne in the first
place? It would be easy to blame the machinations of Edward
of England, but would not John Hastings have made a better
puppet?

John has been maligned and has been made a scapegoat
for the problems of Scotland in the last years of the thirteenth
century. Probably he was no more than a man, sensible of
his rights, who found himself out of his depth when accorded those rights. It required a man of iron to balance
Scottish and English interests.

In 1295 John asserted himself. Repudiating fealty to Edward, he made a secret league with France and, with Edward
occupied on his Welsh campaigns, seized the estates of those
claimants who had not supported his nomination. Alas,
Scottish resurgence, or John's courage, was short-lived; by
the following summer the English army had arrived at
Berwick, laid waste to the countryside and defeated John at
Dunbar. In the second week of July, John abdicated at
Brechin and was despatched, together with the coronation
stone of Scone and the Scottish regalia, to Westminster. For
three years he remained a prisoner in England, eventually
being suffered to leave for France, where he died on his
estates in 1313.

Edward did not replace him with a more compliant competitor. Scotland was placed under the rule of three English
administrators and the throne was to be considered removed
to Westminster: 'it eases one to be rid of dirt' is the alleged
comment of the English king. Henceforth, Scotland was to
be an extension of England, not even thought worthy to be
included in Edward's titles. Truly it might be said that there

54

was 'no longer any king except Edward . . . Arthur himself never had it so fully.'

Among those who marched with Edward to subdue John Balliol's brief independence were two Bruces, son and grandson of the old claimant who died shortly after Balliol's election. The younger Robert, future King of Scotland, was about twenty-two years of age and, since the death of his mother in 1292, had been Earl of Carrick, a title today borne by the Prince of Wales.[24] The mother, Marjorie, had inherited the Carrick estates on the death of her father in 1256 and, in the custom of the time, the title had been held by two husbands in succession: the first, Adam de Kilconrath, dying on crusade, the second being young Robert's father who made over his interests to his son, together with his claim to the throne, in 1291.

The preponderance of Roberts in the Bruce family has invariably caused confusion for chroniclers and historians, ancient and modern, and I can do no better than follow the sensible precedent of Sir Leslie Stephen, editor of the *Dictionary of National Biography*, in numbering them from the time of their arrival in England. This makes the old claimant Robert Bruce VI and his grandson, the future king, Robert Bruce VIII. (Also, in future chapters, when talking of the grandson, I have omitted the prefix 'de'. It was not in general use by historians and appears superfluous after he became King of Scots.)

One tradition maintains that the family descended from 'Thebotaw, Duke of Sleswick and Stosmasch', who flourished in the middle of the eighth century, the surname being derived from Brusi, joint-Earl of the Orkneys in the eleventh century and half-brother to Thorfinn.[25] Such tradition is romantic but groundless: the name is almost cer-

55

tainly derived from the castle and lands of Bruis, now Brix, between Cherbourg and Vallonges, from where Robert de Bruse, 'a noble Norman knight', followed William of Normandy to England in 1066. His son, Robert de Bruce II, who died about 1141, was a companion of the future David I of Scotland at the English court, and when David ascended the throne in 1124 Robert received the lands of Strath Annet, later called Annandale, embracing much of Dumfriesshire. The new lord of Annandale also had extensive interests in England – and loyalty to two monarchs. Failing in an attempt to prevent his Scottish patron from invading England in support of Matilda – the invasion culminating in the Battle of the Standard – Bruce renounced Annandale and retired to his estates in Cleveland, where he founded a monastery of canons regular at Guisburn, now Guisborough. Four centuries later, Margaret Tudor, widow of James IV, erected the Bruce cenotaph in the monastery, a memorial which today stands, engraved with effigies of the early Bruces, in Guisborough parish church.

In 1166 Annandale was restored to Robert Bruce III, known as *Le Meschin*, the cadet, and he strengthened the Scottish ties by marrying a daughter of William the Lion. By the time their grandson, the old competitor, was pressing his claim to the throne, the family had become one of the most powerful in the island and there is no need for putative descent from shadowy rulers of Sleswick or from an Orkney *jarl* with a fortuitious name. Of course, such tradition exists in most noble houses, particularly those with Celtic blood or connections. Brian Boru claimed descent from the third century hero, Fionn mac Cumhaill; while Norse and Saxon kings claimed Wodin as a common ancestor. In more recent days, newly created Victorian peers brought a pedigree commensurate with their title and found it obligatory to have at least one ancestor a 'companion-in-arms' to William of Normandy. An illuminating example is that of the Irish family of Mullins which, elevated to the peerage, Normanised itself as de Molyneux. It is interesting to note that, today, the male representatives of the Bruces, who hold the seventeenth-century earldom of Elgin, begin their pedigree simply, with a 'near relative of the Bruce kings' in 1334.[26]

That the Bruces were, in modern parlance, 'worth cultivating' by the thirteenth century is apparent from the abduction of the competitor's eldest son by the widowed Marjorie of Carrick. She carried him off to her castle of Turnberry in Ayrshire and married him in secret. The tale is worth repeating in the words of Fordun:[27]

After she had become mistress of her father's domain, as she was one day going out hunting at random, with her esquires and handmaidens, Marjorie met a knight riding across the same country – a most seemly youth, named Robert of Bruce, son of Robert, surnamed the Bruce, the noble lord of Annandale in Scotland and of Cleveland in England. When greetings and kisses had been given on each side, as is the wont of courtiers, she besought him to stay and hunt, and walk about; and seeing that he was rather unwilling to do so, she by force, so to speak, with her own hand, made him pull up, and brought the knight, although very loath, to her castle . . . After dallying there, with his followers, for the space of fifteen days or more, he clandestinely took the countess to wife; while the friends and well-wishers of both knew nothing about it, nor had the king's consent been got at all in the matter . . .

One can understand Robert's reticence. His own lands, as well as those of Turnberry, were placed at risk by marrying without the king's consent. Alexander III did seize Turnberry but, 'by means of the prayers of friends, and by a certain sum of money agreed upon', he forgave the couple, although his disapproval of the marriage may have been the reason for the Bruces' failing to gain the prominence in royal circles they had held briefly in the time of Alexander II. Robert Bruce VI said the old king had made him heir presumptive in 1238; and, after the deaths of Alexander III's sons and until it could be seen whether or not Queen Yolande was *enceinte*, it would have been logical for a Bruce to be recognised as heir presumptive. That Alexander III made no provision for a line of succession in the event of the deaths of his daughter or grand-daughter in Norway suggests that, despite the 'certain sum of money', the Bruces were out of favour for many years.

No seer was at hand to prophesy that the first and second sons of that clandestine marriage would become kings: that one would eventually sit upon Alexander's throne, or that the other would find himself a crown in the land of his ancestor, Brian Boru.[28]

CHAPTER THREE

Brothers in Arms

Where the future Bruce kings of Scotland and Ireland were born is uncertain. Although the date of Robert's birth is generally agreed as being 11th July 1274, the place has been described variously as the castle of Turnberry in Ayrshire, Lochmaben in Dumfriesshire and Writtle in Essex.[1] An English birthplace has the support of Fordun, although the manor of Writtle, near Chelmsford, which had been part of the Bruce estate before the family developed Scottish connections in the twelfth century, was by no means their principal seat. Indeed, Robert de Bruce of La Bruse in Normandy, who may be regarded as the first proven ancestor of King Robert, had died in 1094 possessed of forty thousand acres of English soil; including forty-three manors in the West and East Ridings of Yorkshire and fifty-one in the North Riding and in Co. Durham, the most important being Skelton in Cleveland.[2]

By 1274 the family had for more than a century held the Annandale fief from the Scottish kings; Robert Bruce VI, grandfather of the future king, had established his seat at Lochmaben Castle and his son's romantic abduction had brought the old Carrick seat of Turnberry into the family.

As already noted, one source of confusion for historians

throughout the centuries has been the use of Robert as a Christian name among the Bruces. The old competitor and his grandson have been consistently muddled: indeed, several historians have claimed that they were one and the same person, and that the eighteen-year-old Robert had served on the council of regency after the death of Alexander III. The tradition of Writtle as young Robert's birthplace has doubtless come about because of his grandfather's role in English politics. The competitor, as we have seen, served as a Justice of the King's Bench, fought for Henry III at the Battle of Lewes in 1264 and, by his marriage in 1244 to Isabel, daughter of Gilbert de Clare, Earl of Gloucester, joined himself to one of the most powerful families in England.

However, by 1274 he was involved closely in Scottish affairs, and, while his claim to have been heir presumptive to Alexander II does not appear to have been taken seriously by anyone else, it presumably was convenient, in pressing his claim, to live on his Scottish estates.

So it must have been at Lochmaben or Turnberry that his grandsons were born, Edward following Robert after an interval of uncertain length although it could have been no later than 1280, as all accounts of his life suggest that he was reasonably close in age to his brother.

As grandsons of a powerful nobleman, the young Bruces would have led a childhood typical of their rank and of the period. Castles of stone had appeared in Scotland during the days of Alexander II and III, the builders influenced by the Norman blood and traditions flowing in the veins of so many of the Scottish nobility, and what is probably the oldest castle in the country, Castle Sween in Argyllshire,[3] is pure Norman in construction. Said to have been built by the lords of Craignish early in the thirteenth century, and destroyed only in 1645, its great rectangular buttresses were of a style common south of the border. Lochmaben, destroyed in 1384 and rebuilt nearby a century later, only to be destroyed again during the Catholic rising of Lord Maxwell in 1588, was a masterpiece of Norman engineering and architecture. Four miles west of modern-day Lockerbie, on a peninsula in Castle Loch, its walls enclosed sixteen acres, beyond which were four concentric moats. All that remains of what was regarded as the strongest fortress in the Lowlands is a large motte overlooking the town of Lochmaben, founded by the Bruces and which, through the centuries, was enlarged by stones plundered from the ruined castle.

The town is small – there are fewer than one and a half thousand inhabitants – and in the days of Robert Bruce VI what would then have been a collection of wooden buildings below the castle housed the overflow of castle servants and the workers on the demesne lands of Annandale, of which Lochmaben remains the capital. The wide High Street of today probably follows the lines of the original and, in the centre, would have risen the stone cross around which the local market was held and beneath which itinerant friars preached the Gospels. The present church is Georgian, although the bell has traditional associations with King Robert Bruce; and while there was an earlier building on the site, burned in the sixteenth century with many of the Clan Maxwell inside, there is no evidence that a church existed in the days of the Bruces. Their spiritual needs would have been met by the castle chaplain and confessor.

Life for young Robert and Edward, and, in time, their three brothers, doubtless revolved around the martial arts and the chase. Hunting, fishing, fencing, jousting, hawking, bear-baiting and chess-playing were amusements of the day for those who lived among 'draughty rush-strewn halls and tiny stone-walled closets in mingled splendour and discomfort'.[4] They were brought up to speak Norman-French as a first language, for the Scottish aristocracy were as remote from their Celtic subjects as were the Norman and Angevin kings from their Saxons. While in Ireland the 'Old English' – the de Burghs, FitzGeralds, Joyces and others – quickly adapted or adopted Irish speech, customs and dress, the Bruces and Balliols took longer to assume the colour of the country. The Scottish court had been a replica of Westminster since the time of David I, as much an English earl as a Celtic king, who surrounded himself with companions from the southern kingdom. Certainly, Gaelic would have been known, learned from wet-nurses and castle servants and, because of the source, spoken with heavy regional accents. Latin was spoken as a matter of course through religious services and by those in authority, because it was the language of the law and of civilised Europe. Edward Bruce's obituary in the anonymous *Battle of Fochart of St Bridget* notes his 'skill in the various languages of Europe' and his 'acquaintance with the liberal sciences', and certainly there remains the tradition of King Robert, hunted in the heather, amusing his tired band of followers by reading to them from a French romance, or *chanson*.

Doubtless, the brothers would have heard and learned the northern English dialect which, in time, was to become the common speech from Strathclyde to the borders and from Lothian to the seaports on the eastern coast. A trilingual accomplishment at an early age was to prove invaluable to both Robert and Edward in later life, seeking support as they did from three spheres.

At the age of ten or twelve a boy of the station of Robert and Edward was sent as a page to some noble lady, where he might learn courtesy; then to a high-ranking friend of his father for whom he attended at table and carried out other services before becoming a squire and looking after his master's arms.

The days of sending a boy away to a monastery for his education – Brian Boru and his brothers were taught by the monks at Innisfallen in the Irish lakeland of Killarney – were long gone; and it was not until the reign of James IV (1488–1513) that the Scottish barons and gentry were commanded to send their sons to school from the age of eight or nine until they became good Latin scholars.[5]

To become 'a good and faithful knight', to swear to defend the weak and eschew any act of dishonour, was the ambition of every son of a noble house; to bear oneself well in the list at tournament and, in turn, on the field of battle was more glorious than the ability to learn to read Latin manuscripts.

Robert and Edward doubtless attended the court of King Alexander as pages, even though the senior members of their family were out of favour, their close connection with the royal house providing them with the opportunity to learn their lessons from the highest source. But Alexander died in 1286 when Robert was twelve and Edward perhaps nine, so that it was in their grandfather's household at Lochmaben that the boys began their training in earnest. Certainly the old competitor was far more an influence in their lives than their father: Robert Bruce VII after his abduction by, and marriage to, the heiress of Carrick had little part to play in his country's history. In everything, he followed his father's lead without question, even to the point of surrendering his own right to the throne in favour of his eighteen-year-old son. His friendship with Edward of England, and his refusal to take part in Balliol's attempt to overthrow English power in 1295, resulted in the temporary loss of his estates; and after Edward had 'rid himself of the dirt' in Scotland Bruce retired to England, serving briefly as governor of Carlisle and taking no further interest in his northern estates.

At Easter, 1304, he died and was buried at the abbey of Holmcultram in Cumberland.[6] It is difficult to take seriously the story, told by Fordun and repeated by later historians, that after Balliol's abdication Bruce himself claimed the Scottish crown 'in fulfilment of a promise' made, presumably, by King Edward. Indeed, Edward's supposed comment,

> Ne avons ren autres chos a fere
> Que a vous reaulmes ganere?

suggests that the king had small regard for Bruce. More likely the tale was concocted so that the Bruce claim to the throne would appear continuous if, for the moment, unsuccessful.

From an early age, Robert and Edward knew of their close links with the royal house of Scotland: perhaps they cherished adolescent dreams of kingship, although one wonders whether they regarded themselves as Scotsmen. Certainly they were never in the position of the 'Old English' magnates of Ireland among whom, even as late as the reign of Henry VIII, only one had any idea of what was being recited in English during the proclamation of Henry as King of Ireland.

At the age of twenty, Robert Bruce was a man of consequence. Already Earl of Carrick on the death of his mother and the surrender of his father's claim to the title, he now became lord of Annandale and master of extensive estates on both sides of the border. In 1294 the old competitor had died, full of years and honours, and was buried at Guisburn in Cleveland, where his ancestor had founded the monastery of canons regular in the twelfth century. Disappointed

The Grianan of Aileach, in modern Co. Donegal, was the headquarters of the Ui Néill kingdom of Aileach. Domhnall Ui Néill welcomed Edward Bruce to Ireland in 1315. (*Irish Tourist Board*)

Robert Bruce in combat with Sir Henry de Bohun before the Battle of Bannockburn, from an eighteenth-century engraving. (*Mary Evans Picture Library*)

though he may have been in his pretensions to kingship, the lord of Annandale was potent and formidable in his last years. The grandsons must early in life have been aware of the opportunities awaiting them, and perhaps the old man saw in one of them the means of retrieving the family prestige.

The first opportunity came in 1296. Edward of England was at war again with Philip of France and had embarked upon a costly campaign in Flanders, to the displeasure of many of his barons who had small interest in helping the king regain territories in France, and who saw his attempts to raise an army without the aid of the traditional feudal levy as an attack on their own power. If Edward could command all £20 freeholders to serve in Flanders (a scheme he later abandoned) without formally summoning an army under the customary procedure, how long would it be before other aspects of the system were altered to the king's will?

Edward's preoccupation with France provided another man in Scotland with opportunity. William Wallace, the son of a small landowner in Renfrewshire, together with a band of companions, many of them outlawed by Edward, attacked and massacred the English garrison in Lanark. Fearful of rebelling themselves, yet now more frightened by royal incursions on their feudal privileges, many of the Scottish nobles sided with Wallace. Among them was the young Earl of Carrick.

The rebellion, as far as Bruce was concerned, appears to have been a protest at the increasing powers of his overlord, King Edward; and when a force sent northwards by the king overtook the lords on the Ayrshire coast Robert and the others capitulated. The one condition they made for future good behaviour was that they should not be sent to fight in France.[7] It seems strange, and is destructive of the traditional

picture of a medieval nobleman, one who was always ac-
coutred for war. Perhaps tradition has ignored the fact that
personal aggrandisement is not built on war or acts of chivalry, and that these accepted hallmarks of the time were
often greatly exaggerated. Of course, the feudal system survived – Edward I was eulogised after his death as the em-
bodiment of the system, although he used it to suit his own
ends – and one can only assume that Bruce had good reasons
for not wishing to leave Scottish soil.

Wallace continued to fight. Like Brian Boru in Clare, three
centuries earlier, he organised a guerrilla campaign unprecedented in Scottish history. Unlike Brian, he had a
peasantry on whom to fall back for support, for shelter, for
food. If the nobles had been annoyed by Edward's attitude
to their feudal rights, the ordinary people in the glens and
the forests of Selkirk and the wild, trackless land north of the
Tay had been infuriated by the king's attempts to make them
part of that alien system. 'A new phenomenon . . . had
appeared to confront the centralising encroachments of
great organisers and legalists like Edward . . . it was to
become known as patriotism . . .'[8] William Wallace, the poor
knight from Renfrewshire, was indeed a patriot; he had
few lands, no important sinecure at court, no estates in England and no claim to a crown. But he had a love for his
country.

Throughout the summer of 1297, he wore down English
opposition. The victory at Stirling Bridge on 11th September
of that year saw the rout of an English army led by the Earl
of Surrey. The castles of Dundee and Stirling surrendered to
Wallace and by the end of the year only three castles, Dunbar, Edinburgh and Roxburgh, remained in the hands of an
English garrison. By the spring of 1298 Scotland was virtually an independent state again, and how different Sur-

rey's campaign had been compared with that led by a subsequent Earl of Surrey, a little over two centuries later, which culminated in the Battle of Flodden.

The Flanders campaign proved a failure and in March 1298 Edward returned to England, marching northwards and establishing his court at York. Rather than waste his time on vainglorious attempts to recapture the Angevin empire of his great-grandfather, Henry II, he determined now to consolidate his rule in Britain. Wallace had been declared guardian of the kingdom of Scotland in the name of King John Balliol, who languished in England, and had ravaged Cumberland and Northumberland; and while many of the Scottish nobles had remained neutral, despising the lowly Wallace, Edward realised that it might only be a matter of time before they threw in their lot with him. Scotland as a nation might mean little to them, but power meant a great deal and Wallace's success could bring power.

Initially, Edward summoned the Scottish lords to York, a summons refused although still the nobles did not side openly with Wallace. Among the recalcitrants, once more, was Robert Bruce, Earl of Carrick. Was he again protesting against what he regarded as the king's bureaucratic policy of subjugating the feudal system, or were plans of kingship forming in his mind?

The war continued. Ignoring the nobles, Edward concentrated on Wallace, although it was not until 22nd July 1298 that the two forces met. At the Battle of Falkirk, Edward's bowmen destroyed Wallace's army as surely as a later generation of archers was to destroy the French at Agincourt in 1415. Edward had discovered the power of the 'stiff, large and strong bow' during his Welsh campaign and it was Welsh mercenaries who now shot down the schiltrons, or shield troops, of Wallace, the cavalry being powerless to break them. Wallace escaped the slaughter and, with a handful of men, fled into the woods of Callander.

Scotland was not yet subdued. Wallace, the lowly knight, was summarily dismissed as guardian of the realm, his place taken by Balliol's nephew, John Comyn, 'the Red', whose father had been a competitor for the throne, and by Robert Bruce.

Edward's army, worn out by the campaign, many of the soldiers having barely rested since returning from Flanders, was mutinous. The king made one attempt to chastise Bruce and found the castle of Ayr, where he hoped to surprise the earl and gather much-needed supplies, burned to the ground. Bruce, emulating Wallace, melted into the hills and Edward marched wearily back to England.

Was Bruce fighting for Scotland or for himself? For the next five years, with one exception, he resisted Edward, defying two further English invasions and retaining 'guardianship of the realm' in John Balliol's name. He was opposing his feudal overlord and, at the same time, supporting his overlord's erstwhile choice for the throne. There seemed little possibility of John Balliol ever returning to Scotland and, had Edward made the equally unlikely move of recognising Scottish independence, John Comyn, the ex-king's nephew, had a strong claim to the throne. Was Bruce still uncertain of his own support? Was he waiting for the right moment to put forward his own claim?

Early in 1303 England and France signed a treaty and Edward could thus turn his attentions north of the border. Having granted foreign merchants trading with England an impressive charter, freeing them from tolls, receiving in return increased duties on certain imports and exports, the king could finance a strong force of invasion and between

June and September 1303 made short work of Scottish resistance.

Robert Bruce once more made his peace with Edward and in 1305 attended parliament at Westminster as an English baron. The same year, William Wallace was betrayed to the English, tried in Westminster Hall and hanged, drawn and quartered at Smithfield. His rebellion might never have been: an administrative council for the governance of Scotland was appointed, Robert Bruce taking his place with other lords, temporal and spiritual, and the stage was set for Scotland to become an integral part of Edward's realm of Britain.

Bruce was now serving the bureaucracy defied by Wallace and which he had himself defied. His apparent change of heart may be explained by his marriage, in 1302, to Elisabeth, daughter of no less a magnate than Richard de Burgh, Earl of Ulster.[9] It had brought him far closer to the English king, for Elisabeth's mother had been a cousin of Eleanor of Castile, Edward's first and much-loved wife. Even more, it provided Bruce with an important link with affairs in Ireland and with a father-in-law whose power in Ireland nearly equalled that of Edward in England.

Was the marriage another step in Robert's hesitant path to the throne? Risks in the past had paid dividends: forsaking Wallace, although assuming his mantle as guardian, he had made himself leader of an Anglo-Norman clique in Scotland and, when the time was right, submitted dutifully to the feudal overlord. Rebellion resulted not only in pardon but in high office, while for Wallace and others it led to forfeiture and the gallows. Bruce's estates were intact, and his power as a member of the advisory council was considerable. Alliance with the lord of Ulster could bring fresh reward.

On 11th February 1306 Bruce's intrigues could be con-

EDWARD BRUCE

cealed no longer. During a meeting with his fellow-counsellor and recent fellow guardian, John Comyn, in the church of the Greyfriars at Dumfries, Bruce drew his sword and cut Comyn down on the steps of the high altar. Whether or not he emerged from the church exclaiming: 'I doubt I ha' slain the Red Comyn', and whether or not his servants, waiting in the churchyard, declared: 'We'll mak sicker' and finished off the work, does not matter. What is important is the reason for Bruce and Comyn meeting in the first place. Was Bruce, as more than one historian has suggested,[10] plotting rebellion against Edward and trying to persuade Comyn to join him? Did Comyn threaten to denounce the plot, or even put forward his own unquestionable claim to the throne? Tracing Bruce's pendulum-like swings of loyalties in the past, and his readiness to accept office under the authority of the moment, makes one suspicious. He can hardly have thought to escape the king's notice when, in a second, he committed murder and sacrilege. If he was ready to discard completely his allegiance to Edward, his action in the Greyfriars church left him with no future option. Pardoned three times by Edward for defiance, he knew now that there would be no escape from retribution.

At once he imprisoned the royal judges who happened to be on assize in Dumfries and marched to Scone, where, having received absolution from Bishop Wishart of Glasgow, an old friend and one-time regent of Scotland, he was crowned king on Palm Sunday. A local blacksmith hurriedly fashioned a golden circlet for the ceremony, the Scottish regalia having been taken to England together with the coronation stone, and it was placed on Robert's head by Isabella, Countess of Buchan, sister of the Earl of Fife. The countess, who may have been Robert's mis-

70

tress,[11] symbolised the ancient and hereditary right of her family to crown a Scottish king: it was a brilliant move by Robert.

There was no chance of pardon this time. 'He is a traitor and our enemy,' declared Edward, when he heard the news. The Earl of Pembroke, commander of the English army in Scotland, was ordered to burn Bruce's manors, 'to destroy his lands and goods and to strip his gardens clean so that nothing is left, for an example to others like him'.

Also, there was far from universal support for the new king among his subjects. While most people might have welcomed a king of their own again, the awful deed in Greyfriars set many potential supporters against Robert. 'All the commons went him fra', according to an old rhyme, and doubtless there were many who recalled the curse of St Malachy, laid on the house of Bruce in 1148.

The saint, then Archbishop of Armagh, was journeying from Ireland to Rome and had spent the night at the Annandale house of the second Robert de Bruce. Discovering that shortly before his arrival a thief had been captured and was then awaiting sentence, Malachy asked, as a boon from his host, that the man's life be spared. This was agreed and he blessed the household, only to see the thief dangling from the gallows next morning. Infuriated by the apparent duplicity of the lord of Annandale, the saint revoked his blessing and laid a perpetual curse on the family. Over a century later, Robert the competitor attempted to remove what was generally seen as a major disability. Several times he made a pilgrimage to the saint's tomb, praying for the curse to be lifted, and in 1272, returning from the Holy Land, he confirmed by charter a perpetual rent 'to God and the Blessed Mary and to the house and monks of Clairvaux in order to maintain lights before the blessed Malachy and for the good

71

of his own soul and the souls of his predecessors and successors'.

Any benediction received as a result was negated, in the fourteenth-century mind, by the murder at Greyfriars; and by the end of 1306 the new King of Scotland was almost alone, wandering as Wallace had wandered, finally seeking refuge on the island of Rathlin, off the coast of northern Ireland. There, in a cave, the legend of the spider was born[12] and there, it seemed, the king would starve to death. Most of his supporters had been captured and hanged, although his brother Edward is said by many sources to have escaped to Rathlin with him; his wife was a prisoner in England and no help was forthcoming from his father-in-law, Richard de Burgh, whose territories could be seen across the four miles of sea separating Rathlin from the mainland. Richard, for all his ruthlessness, could not succour one who had committed the worst form of sacrilege, as a result of which his daughter was now incarcerated in England.

And what of Edward Bruce at this time? History, if not legend, is silent about him until 1307, but it does seem likely that he shared the Rathlin cave. Had he remained in Scotland it is difficult to imagine that he could have survived the general slaughter or imprisonment of his family. Three younger brothers, Sir Nigel Bruce, Sir Thomas Bruce and Alexander Bruce, Dean of Glasgow (whose influence perhaps helped Bishop Wishart salve his conscience and grant Robert absolution), were taken and hanged, drawn and quartered. Their sisters, Mary, wife of Sir Nigel Campbell, and Christian, wife of Sir Christopher de Seton[13] were also captured; Lady de Seton was confined at Sixhill Priory in Lincolnshire, while Lady Campbell was imprisoned, allegedly in an iron cage, first at Roxburgh Castle, then at

Newcastle, together with the Countess of Buchan, who had crowned Robert. Mary was to be exchanged for English prisoners in 1312 and Christian was released in 1314, but for the moment they seemed doomed to imprisonment for life. Fordun, in a vivid passage, says that in 1306 Robert's friends in Scotland were 'as a single drop compared with the waves of the sea, or as a single grain of seed compared with the multitudinous sand', in comparison with his enemies. To those enemies might be added others, nobles and peasants, who, appalled by Comyn's murder, were yet more appalled at the treatment meted out to the Bruce family. If any other descendants of the original competitors had once harboured ideas of one day gaining the throne for themselves, the apparent end of the house of Bruce turned fond dreams into nightmares.

It is with difficulty that we sympathise with Robert at this point in his career. Having vacillated in the past, he appears 'a typical Anglo-Norman baron in quest of aggrandisement', as one writer has called him.[14] His sudden declaration of independence had been forced upon him by a particularly savage murder in sacred precincts, and one cannot help but wonder whether Comyn's death was caused not by sudden anger, or fear of betrayal, but by a carefully planned action to eliminate the only other man with sufficient prestige to claim or seize the throne himself. It seems strange that Robert would have taken Comyn, a rival for the crown, into his confidence if he was plotting insurrection, although, as we have seen, this has been given as a reason for the murder. One can, of course, take the view that Robert simply bided his time until he could strike hard against the English and that John Comyn's death was an accident, caused in a momentary flush of anger or frustration. Scotland, at the time of the crime, appeared utterly subdued by the English:

had Comyn not died, had the meeting not occurred, would Robert still have taken the crown? Certainly the possible outcome – forfeiture, the imprisonment of his wife and sisters and the ignominious death of three of his brothers – had materialised.[15] Edward Bruce, alone of his near relations, was with him and the blood of more than Comyn was on his hands.

In later years, Edward Bruce was to act no less an 'Anglo-Norman baron in search of aggrandisement', but for now his fate was interwoven with that of his brother and, for a time at least, Edward was to prove an able lieutenant. But since the age of fifteen or so, from the time Robert had become Earl of Carrick, representative of his family's regnal pretensions, Edward lived in his brother's shadow. His resentment of the fact was to appear later.

Edward had married by the time the brothers arrived on Rathlin. His wife was Isabel, daughter of Earl Dawy of Athol, and while nothing is known of her, it appears she was incapable of bearing children. Edward was to leave three sons,[16] all of them by his mistress, Ysabella, daughter of William, Earl of Ross, with whom his affair may have started by 1306. That all three sons were of age to bear arms and take part in campaigns against the English by the 1330s suggests that they were born no later than 1310, probably earlier. In 1317 Pope John XXII was to grant a dispensation to Edward and Ysabella to marry, although they were 'in the third and fourth degrees of consanguinity', for the purpose of 'putting an end to the feuds between their parents, relations and friends'. Edward's parents, of course, were long dead by 1317 and one questions the suggestion of righteous indignation felt by the old Earl of Ross at the sight of his daughter living as concubine to the king's brother.

As it happened, Edward died before the marriage could

take place, but all three sons were to inherit the earldom of Carrick in turn and, as we shall see later, were acknowledged by their uncle as being heirs in line to the throne.

The earldom was made over to Edward Bruce by Robert at the time of the coronation, but it was an empty honour with Turnberry in English hands. The future offered capture and execution or starvation on Rathlin.

Whether or not the spider story is true – to Sir Walter Scott, the legend suited well his image of Bruce as a Christian knight – the brothers took new heart, or at least a calculated risk, and in February 1307 reappeared at Turnberry, trying unsuccessfully to capture the English governor. Gathering round them a small group of friends, including their nephew, Sir Thomas Randolph and, most notable of all, Sir James Douglas, the 'Black Douglas' of romance, they emulated the despised Wallace. Surprise attacks on outlying English garrisons were followed by concealment in the wilderness: the tactics of the guerrilla through the ages began first to irritate, then to wear down, the English forces.

Douglas, who was to remain a close friend of Robert until the king's death and was himself to die fighting against the Saracen with Bruce's heart in a casket around his neck, is a real hero of the time. As Bruce's followers had melted away after the English invasion, so they reassembled at Douglas's call. 'Stouter was he than a leopard,' it was said of Douglas (as, indeed, it was to be of Edward Bruce), and it was his gallantry, rather than a spider, which surely gave Robert the impetus necessary to regain the throne.

By 10th May 1307 a sufficient force had gathered to meet the English in battle. We know from Fordun and other sources that Edward Bruce was present when, at Loudoun Hill in Ayrshire, Lord Pembroke was routed. Within a week, another force under the Earl of Gloucester had been defeated and as success followed surprising success other Scottish nobles flocked to the new king's standard.

Success was all the more surprising because half the country stood aloof from Robert. Early in July, Edward of England left Carlisle at the head of a formidable army and, had he reached his destination, even the courage of Douglas would have been hard-pressed to withstand him.

But on 7th July, within marching distance of the Scottish border, 'Edward the Great, king of the Saxons, and of Britain, and of Alba, and duke of Gascony, and lord of Erinn, *quievit in Christo* in the thirty-fifth year of his reign, and in the sixty-sixth year of his age . . .'[17] Edward, Hammer of the Scots, was dead, his last words a command to his successor that his bones be carried before the army as it continued its march northward.

Had Robert waited another year or eighteen months before declaring himself king, would the sequel have been different? While it is useless to speculate on the possibilities of history, it is certain that King Edward was unwell for a year before his death, and the end, had it come at Westminster rather than in camp at Burgh-on-Sands, could hardly have been long delayed. The old king's heir, gentle, pliant Edward II, had none of his father's energy for campaigning and no real ambition to conquer the Scottish wilderness; and a declaration of independence by Robert, and the imprisonment of his rival, Comyn, would certainly have met with greater support in Scotland had it come at the time of Edward I's death.

As it was, the new English king's decision to abandon the invasion enabled Robert to collect his forces and deal with internal foes, rather than invaders. In 1308, with Edward Bruce, he marched into Galloway, dealing mercilessly with any who opposed him or showed reluctance to join him.[18]

Although still 'a king in the heather', or 'King Hobbe in the Mure' as the English termed him with a humour that was to contribute to their undoing, Robert continued to build up an army; and with no sign of attack he grew bolder. Many who joined him were clansmen of outlaws like James Douglas, who had nothing to lose but a life already fraught with danger and uncertainty. Robert's erstwhile tenants in Carrick joined him rather than languish beneath the Englishmen to whom the estates had been given; and, while many of Robert's followers must have been composed of men pressed into service, the inherent love of the Celt for a battle would have been inspiration enough for many more.

Edward II, meanwhile, was preoccupied with his favourite, the Gascon Piers Gaveston. When, by the summer of 1309, the barons forced him to banish Gaveston,[19] the Bruces were in control of most of Scotland north of the River Tay. In the spring of that year, Edward Bruce, in command after Robert was stricken with fever, won a major victory over a small English force on the Cree; and Robert, recovered, was able to call his first parliament at St Andrews. Quarrels in England between the king and barons over the return of Gaveston proved Scotland's salvation; for, while twenty strongholds were still in English hands, the success of the Bruces was winning new support for the brothers.

Although Robert had been excommunicated after the death of John Comyn, the Scottish clergy, meeting in general council, declared him 'true heir to the crown'. It seems extraordinary, knowing how deeply religious was the Celtic mind, that murder and sacrilege could so easily be forgotten, or that a papal excommunication could be ignored. Indeed, the resistance found in Galloway suggests that not everyone did forget or ignore what had happened, although it must also be remembered that Galloway was the ancestral home of the Balliols through King John's mother, the celebrated and lovely Dervorgilla. The daughter of Alan, last of the Kings of Galloway and, through her mother, a direct descendant of King David I, Dervorgilla is perhaps best remembered as founder of Balliol College, Oxford. In Galloway, at the time of Robert Bruce's punitive expedition, her memory was fresh, albeit for local works of charity rather than for establishing an English college; and as she had died as recently as 1289 there must have been many people who remembered her, and, more importantly, her son's right to the throne.

To the Scottish clergy, however, particularly to those of Norman blood, it was doubtless easier to follow Bishop Wishart's example and support the new king. Unwillingness to accept the dominion of England had already resulted in the Scottish church 'tendering' the kingdom to Pope Boniface VIII in 1300; and the pope, grasping a fresh chance to mediate in earthly monarchy, accepted the offer and ordered Edward I to withdraw his troops, declaring Scotland to be a papal fief. Boniface may have recalled the words of his predecessor, Innocent IV, in reply to the appeal from Henry III of England to confirm the young King Alexander III a liege subject of the English crown. 'To grant such a thing is altogether unheard of,' came the reply from Rome: a decision reversed promptly enough when Henry allowed Innocent the opportunity to dispose of English benefices. Edward I was not to be blackmailed: ordered to 'submit his pretensions' to the apostolic tribunal, he replied furiously that the laws of England did not allow the king to be subject to a foreign tribunal. The Scottish clergy, he maintained, were as much his subjects as their fellows in England; and after Bruce's coronation short shrift was made of Wishart, who was imprisoned in England where blindness was doubtless the least of his troubles.

The support, now, of the clergy may have brought more of the people to Robert. Certainly, two invasion attempts by England in 1310 and 1311 were repulsed and then, in 1312, civil war broke out south of the border.

Taking advantage of this, Robert and Edward Bruce struck again at fortresses still in enemy hands. Edward captured Dundee, his brother marching south as far as Durham, striking terror into the north of England as he went. Perth fell to him in the first week of 1313; Dumfries and the old Bruce stronghold of Lochmaben were surrendered to Edward Bruce in February.

Edward, Earl of Carrick, was undoubtedly winning his spurs, and now it was he who brought the war to a head. Early in 1314 he besieged Stirling Castle, the strongest garrison left to England. The size of his force is unknown, but whether he realised that Stirling might prove impregnable, or whether he acted out of bravado, he bargained with the garrison commander, Sir Thomas Mowbray, that the castle should surrender only if, by midsummer, King Edward had not sent an army to relieve it. Mowbray, delighted at so long a breathing-space and perhaps showing more faith in his king than other men had done, agreed to the terms. Robert was in a quandary: he had insufficient men to take the castle, or to face a large English force, without leaving his dearly won north open to invasion or fresh internal disturbance. Edward Bruce had made a rash bargain: 'Let the King of England bring all the men he has; we will fight them and more,' he is supposed to have answered when taken to task by Robert.[20]

Robert had no choice other than to agree, although the

79

headstrong nature of his brother was to cause further problems in the years to come.

The English took up the challenge. Reluctantly, Edward II set out at the head of 'the greatest army England had ever sent forth',[21] estimated at between two thousand and three thousand knights and twenty thousand archers and spearmen, compared with some seven thousand men, mainly infantry, under Bruce's command.[22] Contingents from Lennox, Mar, Angus, Buchan and Menteith were led by Edward Bruce, Robert commanding a force from the regained lands of Carrick and from the Western Isles, a district always willing to provide doughty fighters. Traditionally, the Highland clans taking part, and serving under their own chieftains, were Cameron, Campbell, Chisholm, Fraser, Gordon, Grant, Gunn, MacKay, MacIntosh, Macpherson, Macquarrie, Maclean, MacDonald, MacFarlane, MacGregor, MacKenzie, Menzies, Munro, Robertson, Ross, Sinclair and Sutherland.

On 23rd June 1314, the Eve of St John, the English arrived at Bannockburn, three miles from Stirling Castle.

The battle was known for generations, both in Scotland and in England, as that of 'the Pools', from the boggy and treacherous nature of the area. Robert's army was drawn up at first on what was then called New Park, high afforested land overlooking the marshes and guarding the main road to Stirling. His force comprised four divisions: Sir James Douglas, with troops from Clydeside and the western borders, on the left; Edward Bruce on the right; Sir Thomas Randolph and men from Ross and Moray in the centre; and the king in reserve behind his brother. In what firm ground there was below New Park, Robert had dug pits, covering them with turf to render them invisible, had planted, as an additional hazard, a network an additional hazard, a network of calthrops, or steel spikes, designed to lame charging horses.[23]

The Scots were awarded an advantage by the condition of the English army. It was exhausted after its march and was troubled with disputes among its commanders. The young Earl of Gloucester, King Edward's nephew (and, through his father, a kinsman of Robert Bruce) had been appointed constable, a move opposed by the Earl of Hereford, who was Hereditary Constable of England and, as such, could claim the honour of leading the vanguard.

King Edward attempted to compromise by naming them joint commanders, but the damage had been done: Gloucester and Hereford were ambitious, distrusting each other and united only with a foolish contempt for the Scottish army. Now, they rejected a plea from Mowbray, inside Stirling, that since the relief force had arrived in good time no battle need take place.[24]

As the English vanguard approached New Park, Robert Bruce was inspecting his troops, not yet expecting a confrontation. He was mounted on a small grey horse and was unarmed except for a battleaxe,[25] and, as such, he was recognised by an English knight, Sir Henry de Bohun, who at once saw an opportunity to create panic among the Scots. Lowering his lance, he charged at Robert, who, at the last moment, turned his horse aside, an easy task on a light mount but impossible for Bohun on his great warhorse.

As the knight thundered past, Bruce rose in his saddle and brought down his axe on Bohun's head, splitting head and helmet in two.

The English advance did not falter. Hereford, who was Bohun's kinsman, and Gloucester pressed forward, but an encounter with the Scots proved indecisive and the English retreated in order.

The real battle was launched soon after daybreak on Midsummer Day. The Scots began the attack, Edward Bruce marching in the formation of a schiltron, or phalanx of spears, forming a thick-set hedge invincible to anything but arrows.[26] Had Edward I been in command of the English army, short work would have been made of the schiltron, but the Earl of Gloucester had already started a cavalry charge and his bowmen were unable to see their target. Gloucester himself was a victim of the charge – Robert Bruce, his kinsman, was to stand vigil over the body, once recovered, until it could be sent back to England – and panic seized the English. Their archers, prevented from firing, unless it was into the backs of their own cavalry, were scattered by a charge of the Scottish horse under Sir Robert Keith; and the heavily armoured English knights, floundering in the bogs and falling into the concealed pits, were easy prey for the Scottish spearmen.

As a body of Bruce's camp followers appeared on the skyline, the English, imagining reinforcements were coming, tried to leave the field. The retreat became a rout and King Edward, who had one horse killed under him and had fought with immense courage, was forced from the melée by his bodyguard. At Stirling Castle, Mowbray refused his sovereign admission: understandably so, as with surrender imminent he could hardly risk the king becoming a hostage. So, closely pursued by James Douglas, the royal party made its way safely to the coast, where a ship took them to the sanctuary of Berwick.

Pembroke, having seen the king off the field, returned to muster what remained of his own contingent, most of them Welshmen. In a little-remembered feat of endurance, he led them home by way of Carlisle, himself barefoot and leading the way on foot towards the end.

Bannockburn was an unmitigated disaster for England and the greatest victory of the period for Scotland. The writer of the *Vita Edwardi Secundi*, recalling the unfortunate king's reign as it drew to a dreadful close, commented: 'Indeed, I think it is unheard of in our time for such an army to be scattered so suddenly by infantry, unless when the flower of France fell before the Flemings at Courtrai.' Courtrai, fought twelve years earlier, had shown that well-armed, disciplined infantry could overcome the potential advantage of heavily armed knights and horses; and while the hidden pits, the naturally boggy terrain at Bannockburn and the inability of the English bowmen to aim clearly at their targets all contributed to the Scottish victory, the battle can be seen as an evolution in the role of the infantry.

Besides the ordinary soldiers who died that day, seven hundred knights and scores of English noblemen fell in battle or drowned in the bogs or the tidal waters of the River Forth as they tried to escape. Five hundred men of rank were made prisoner and, for the next year, were exchanged for the Scots taken hostage in 1306. Among those who came home to Scotland were Robert's wife, Queen Elisabeth de Burgh, and his daughter, the Lady Marjorie, and old Bishop Wishart of Glasgow, blind but undaunted.

Edward Bruce, whose rashness had resulted in a glorious victory, had won his spurs.

CHAPTER FOUR

A Great Fleet-host

Edward Bruce, according to the historian Leland,[1] was of 'a high courageous spirit, chivalrously ambitious of fame in fight, and aspiring to dominion fought abreast with his brother in establishing him on the throne of Scotland; on which he was scarcely firmly placed when Edward demanded to be admitted to an equal share in his authority . . .'

How accurately are we to judge this statement? Inasmuch as chivalry and ambition are concerned, Edward's actions between 1308 and 1314 suggest that he was ambitious for his brother's aspirations to the throne, and his treatment of the besieged garrison at Stirling seems to confirm the suggestion that he was chivalrous. (It might equally suggest caution, especially as we know nothing of the size of his forces at the time.)

Of course, chivalry was too often a cloak concealing ruthlessness and cunning. As an example, Richard I, Coeur de Lion, seen by so many historians as the mirror of knightly behaviour, the epitome of the chivalrous medieval king, could be bestial and cruel. He might have commanded that the archer who gave him the mortal wound at the siege of Châlus be spared (which he was not), but he also committed

84

the most appalling deeds when subduing Cyprus in 1191.[2] Doubtless chivalry was in the eye of the beholder, and the fact that Leland garnered his comments on Edward and Robert Bruce from the fourteenth-century historian, John of Fordun, for whom the brothers could do no wrong, warns us against taking such character sketches too seriously. Neither brother had shown mercy to opposition or neutrality in Galloway in 1308, and not all those who suffered during Robert's climb to the throne were noblemen or English soldiers. Despite popular romances, it took Robert many years to become regarded as the father of his people; indeed, it can be argued that only after his death, and then through the eulogies of Fordun, did he achieve heroic status. In his lifetime there were many patriotic Scots who would remember only too clearly his early vacillation, his murder of the Red Comyn and his desertion of Wallace.

Edward Bruce cannot have lived and fought with his brother without some of that ambition and ruthlessness rubbing off on him. That he was the only surviving brother made him a potent figure, the more so because at the time of Bannockburn Robert's only child was a daughter of about sixteen. Had Robert died suddenly, the succession of the Lady Marjorie could hardly be contemplated: the last twenty-eight years of misery had been the result of the little Maid of Norway's short-lived inheritance. In 1315 Robert decreed that, failing male heirs of his own body, he should be succeeded by Edward or by one of his three sons, their bastardy conveniently ignored. Only after Edward's line was extinguished should Lady Marjorie gain the throne.[3] Robert's own illegitimate brood was also excluded, although two of them, Robert, who received five hundred marks yearly from the king, and Nigel 'of Carrick', who received an annual thirty pounds, were probably living in 1315.

Yet the bastardy of his nephews surely rankled with the founder of this new dynasty on the Scottish throne. The papal dispensation for Edward and his mistress to marry came too late and, in December 1318, less than two months after Edward's death, the king made his two-year-old grandson, Robert FitzAlan, heir presumptive.[4] It seemed an extraordinary move, for the king's death could have plunged the kingdom into as much confusion as the elevation of the young Marjorie would have done three years before. Heavy with child in March 1316, the girl was killed in a riding accident. Surgeons, conscious of the succession, at once operated and removed the living infant from the dead body. Over half a century later, Robert FitzAlan, crippled for life by the operation, was to become Robert II of Scotland, but only after the death of his grandfather's late-born son, David II.[5] Perhaps, in 1318, Robert Bruce was confident that his son-in-law, the High Steward from whom the luckless house of Stewart was to take its name, would prove an able regent. In the event, fate was to deny the king's own blood an easy succession. David II was to ascend the throne at the age of five and inevitable troubles were to fall on Scotland.

This was in the future; for the present, Robert must find occupation for his brother, for there were signs that the earldom of Carrick[6] and the position of heir presumptive were insufficient for the man whose apparently reckless bargain with the Stirling garrison had resulted in the defeat of the English army. Fordun tells us that Edward 'demanded to be admitted to an equal share' of Robert's authority, while John Barbour, the archdeacon who has been called the father of Scottish poetry,[7] also hints at fraternal dispute. Although the metrical history of Robert Bruce is a blatant eulogy on both brothers and cannot be taken as an impartial account by someone who was only two years old when Edward died, one verse is illuminating:

> The Erle of Carick, Schyr Eduward,
> That stouter was than a libbard,
> And had na will to be in pess,
> Thoucht that Scotland to litill was . . .

In modern parlance, Scotland was not big enough for both of them. Now that the crown was upon his head and the English, for the moment, beaten, could Robert trust Edward? Might there not have arisen a pro-Edwardian faction at court, or in the countryside, a faction which, seeing the country independent, might prefer as its new king someone untainted by sacrilege, yet who had shown himself a doughty warrior? Robert was aware that his own position was not unassailable by internal sources and by the English. There was no guarantee that England would not again attempt to impose its authority on Scotland and, before that time came, the kingdom must be allowed to recover from long years of war; strongholds must be rebuilt, crops replanted and, above all, Scotland must be sufficiently united behind the king to withstand another invasion.

An opportunity to provide Edward Bruce with new glory and, at the same time, to strike a blow at England before she recovered from Bannockburn, was not long in appearing. How far it was engineered by Robert, or how far the victory at Bannockburn was its inspiration, is difficult to assess. The opportunity, nothing less than the invasion of Ireland, could hardly have escaped Robert's attention while he was hiding on Rathlin. He was, after all, aware of the dissension in Ireland, much of it provoked by his father-in-law, Richard de Burgh. There was no other country in which he could canvas support for his own schemes, France having made its peace with England when it provided a new consort for Edward I. However, if once he was King of Scotland Robert could negotiate with dissatisfied Irish leaders, native or Norman, England could be irritated in two places at once.

Three centuries earlier, Ireland had looked to its sister kingdom of Scotland for aid in dealing with internal troubles. In 1014 Malcolm II sent his father-in-law, Brian Boru, a contingent of troops under the Great Steward of Mar to fight at Clontarf; two centuries later Donal Oge O'Donnell had freed his native Tir Conaill, in western Ulster, from Norman and Ui Néill claims by importing a band of Scots mercenaries, known to history as the galoglas. 'Tall fierce footmen, with battleaxes as tall as themselves, clad in helmet and coat of mail, refusing to fly and bearing the brunt of the battle till the last',[8] these Gaelic-Norse warriors from the Scottish Isles were to remain an integral element in Irish warfare until the sixteenth century, every great chieftain maintaining a band of them. Their effigies can be seen on tombs of the period throughout Ireland, their costumes a striking contrast to the linen shirts of the native warriors.

Ulster now looked once more to Scotland. Domhnall Ui Néill, King of Aileach, already having suffered much at the hands of Richard de Burgh, and of the Normans generally, turned to the victor of Bannockburn for help. That, at least, is what tradition tells us: that Robert was invited to invade Ulster and that Domhnall excused his action on the grounds of Ireland being leaderless and without hope of justice from England. The excuse was made in a remonstrance directed to Pope John XXII a year after the Scottish invasion.[9] The document, which will be discussed further, is remarkable and today its authenticity is disputed no less than that of the controversial Bull of Pope Adrian IV which, traditionally, sent the Normans to Ireland in the first place.

It cannot be doubted that Domhnall and his compatriots were impressed by the news of Bannockburn and the independence of Scotland. Nor is it impossible that they had been negotiating with Robert Bruce for military support, for a body of galoglas *par excellence*. Certainly, early in 1315, the king had sent envoys to Ulster with a message that surely delighted Domhnall:

Whereas we and you and our people and your people, free since ancient times, share the same national ancestry and are urged to come together more eagerly and joyfully in friendship by a common language and by common custom, we have sent over . . . the bearers of this letter, to negotiate with you in our name about permanently strengthening and maintaining inviolate the special friendship between us and you, so that with God's will your nation may be able to recover her ancient liberty. Whatever our envoys or one of them may conclude with you in this matter we shall ratify and uphold in future . . .

If genuine, it was a masterpiece of diplomacy, highlighting the ancient lineage (of the Ui Néill, let it be said, rather than the mythical kingdom of all-Ireland) and stressing the Celtic origins that bound Irish and Scot, no matter how loosely. That Robert had little interest in the average Celt is of no importance: an appeal to what today would be called nationalism could hardly be resisted and, in Irish eyes, Edward, Earl of Carrick, could appear as Celtic as any of the Ui Néill.

One modern historian[10] has pointed out that Bruce, although on his father's side a feudal Norman, was descended through his mother from the 'ancient Gaelic kings' of Scotland, and thus 'felt himself able to manage the Irish situation'. Yet this simplifies the picture, suggesting that Robert sympathised genuinely with his 'fellow Celts' of Ulster because of his blood. We know already how diluted that blood had become: the last real Celt to sit on the Scottish throne had been Macbeth. From Malcolm III onwards the kings had been influenced by English (or Norman) fashion, and by the time David I, Robert's nearest royal ancestor, had come to the throne in 1124 the court was Westminster in replica. It might also be noted that Robert's claim to the throne came through his great-grandmother, not his mother, whose own Celtic blood was diluted strongly.

Also, the situation in Scotland was entirely different to that in Ireland, the only common denominator being the Celtic blood of the ordinary people who had little voice in the running of the country. The Scottish nobility, Norman or Normanised, lived in a country which, until 1286, had been a clearly defined kingdom of its own. Even when the Scottish king swore allegiance to the ruler of England, he was still the only king in Scotland. In Ireland, despite English claims to rule the entire island, there were myriad principalities regarding themselves independent of their neighbours, much as Robert regarded Scotland in relation to England. The rulers of these states were either men such as Domhnall Ui Néill or Richard de Burgh who, for all the claims of the shadowy high kings, ruled according to their own laws. The subjugation of Ireland by the Scots could never really have been a serious issue: the division and sub-division of kingship and loyalties had proved a stumbling-block for England, and Robert, having fought hard enough for Scotland, would not have contemplated this larger campaign.

It is unlikely that Domhnall Ui Néill saw Bruce, or his brother, as a potential *Ardri* for Ireland, despite the wording of the remonstrance, even if we believe it. He regarded himself as lawful King of Aileach and a contender for the meaningless high kingship, and he saw in Bruce a means of recovering Ulster at least for his family, perhaps more if Scottish aid proved successful. At the same time, he could hardly fail to realise that Robert, for all his trappings of monarchy (and, if we give it credence, Robert's purported message), was as much a Norman baron as Richard de Burgh. If he contemplated offering Robert a permanent foothold, he had only to look back less than two centuries in Irish history to see what happened to Diarmaid mac Muchadha of Leinster. Diarmaid, denigrated as the cause of Ireland's miseries in his own lifetime,[11] had brought foreigners across the sea to help regain his patrimony, with dire consequences. Perhaps the conscience of a man as desperate as Domhnall could be salved by the thought that most of Robert's men were themselves Celts, not Norman adventurers in search of land and power.

Whatever the hopes and fears of Domhnall Ui Néill and Robert of Scotland, the King of Aileach was in Larne harbour, then known as Olderfleet, to welcome an invading army led by Edward Bruce on 25th May 1315. With Edward were his nephew, Sir Thomas Randolph, a scattering of Scottish knights and what has been called[12] the greatest foreign fleet yet landed in Ireland. Traditionally, six thousand Scottish soldiers, most of them seasoned by the last eight or nine years of campaigning, landed that day in three hundred ships. The figures are staggering, if one considers how large an army for the period it constituted. At Bannockburn, the English army comprised around twenty-five thousand men, the Scottish perhaps seven thousand. The English figure is large, although England was a powerful nation, well trained in war since the first campaigns of Edward I and capable of raising a considerable levy. But even after Bannockburn, Robert had enemies within Scotland: how, in little under a year, could he send six thousand men out of the country in a venture that had to depend on Domhnall of Aileach and his allies providing a reliable reserve of troops? So far, they had been unable to defend their own kingdoms satisfactorily, so that, unless Robert was convinced that Celtic Ireland would flock to his brother's banner, the invasion becomes more a means of removing Edward from temptation at home and less an attempt at Celtic solidarity.

Edward's fleet, whatever its size, impressed the annalists. 'A great fleet-host came from Scotland with the brother of the king of Scotland, that is, with Edward, into the territories of Ulidia,' record the *Annals of Ulster*; 'Edward, son of the Earl of Alba,[13] came to Erinn, on the coast of Uladh in the north, with a fleet of three hundred ships,' we find in the *Annals of Loch Cé*; while the *Annals of Clonmacnoise* confirm the number of ships: 'Edward mcRobert Bruce, earle of Carick and brother of king Robert, king of Scotland, Landed with a fleet of three hundred ships in the north of Ulster; at whose comeing all the Inhabitants of Ireland, both English and Irish, were stricken with great terrour, that it made the Lands and Inhabitants of Ireland to shake for feare . . .'

In all cases, the annalists were writing retrospectively,[14] although the terror and fear provoked by the invasion was real enough in the light of subsequent events. Domhnall Ui Néill and Robert Byset, lord of the Glens of Antrim, a chieftain of Scottish descent who immediately joined Edward, were to learn that their confidence in the invaders was dreadfully misplaced.

It will be as well at this juncture to examine the position in Ireland of the English, as opposed to the Anglo-Irish magnates and the native chieftains. After all, English officialdom, the English 'garrison', might be expected to bear the brunt of the invasion and, should it be successful, the wrath of the English king.

In 1315 the eastern counties of Ireland were enjoying a comparatively peaceful period. Edward I, occupied with Welsh, French and then Scottish wars, had shown scant interest in Ireland, unless it was to raise taxes and levies for those wars. However, he was determined that the island should be as integral a part of his British kingdom as Wales or Scotland, and if this 'hard working and orderly king'[15] had a fault it was the inability to realise that the Celt and Gael had no inclination to accept an orderly administration, no desire to become part of an efficient machinery, and no sense of the common interest which had been maturing slowly among the English since the time of Henry II. That Edward I was far from being a despot, riding roughshod over the hopes and feelings of his inferiors, is evident throughout his long reign. Even the barons, who had proved so troublesome to his father and grandfather, and who were to bring about the deposition and murder of his son, were treated with unusual leniency. That the king thrice pardoned Robert Bruce for refuting his authority is proof enough; and even in Wales he sought methods other than brute force in gaining the friendship and allegiance of the native princes.

His determination to inquire into, and where necessary abolish, the old feudal and episcopal privileges which obstructed officialdom and unification was crystallised in the Statute of Gloucester, passed in 1285 and including Ireland as much as England within its legislation. But it was not until 1295 that officialdom tried with any measure of success to enforce the statute in Ireland. That year, the king appointed as justiciar of the island a Pembrokeshire knight, Sir John de Wogan, whose brief was to end the feuds of the Norman and Celtic nobles and make Ireland an efficient and lucrative part of the kingdom. That, as the *Annals of Clonmacnoise* record, there 'reigned more dissensions, strife, wars and debates between the Englishmen themselves than between the Irishmen' shows the task confronting the new justiciar; and the reconciliation of Richard de Burgh and the FitzGeralds (see page 30) was not the least of his difficulties. Two years after his appointment, Sir John summoned a parliament, calling together in English fashion, and for the first time in Irish history, knights of the shires and representatives of the liberties, or areas of special privileges. Knights came from Dublin, Louth, Waterford, Cork, Tipperary, Limerick, Kerry and Roscommon, and seneschals of the liberties from Meath, Wexford, Carlow, Kilkenny and, somewhat vaguely, Ulster, showing how far the English had penetrated. It is worth comparing the situation with that at the end of the fourteenth century, when the much smaller Pale[16] first appeared as a distinct area of 'safe', or English-held, land.

With two interruptions, John de Wogan was to be justiciar of Ireland until 1312, although his task, carried out conscientiously, was unrewarding. King Edward himself interfered at one stage, granting an erstwhile liberty to his second son, Thomas of Brotherton, thus upsetting the delicate balance between feudalism and bureaucracy; and while another parliament, meeting in Kilkenny in 1309, passed strict laws to repress robbery, particularly that committed by men of noble birth,[17] the high ideal of a parliament legislating for Ireland, rather than for the English in Ireland, had faded. In Connacht, Thomond and elsewhere, internecine disputes, native and Anglo-Irish, continued to disturb the king's peace; and the deteriorating situation was certainly not helped by the arrival of a man who was to rival Richard de Burgh of Ulster.

He was Roger Mortimer, a leading Anglo-Norman lord in

the Welsh Marches with castles at Ludlow and Wigmore. Later to earn notoriety in the deposition and murder of Edward II, Mortimer laid claim to large estates in Meath and Leix, and although, legally, he was entitled to them, he had been too long an absentee and his reappearance caused hostility among his neighbours. Much of Meath was already ruled by the de Lacy and de Verdun families, while in Leix the O'Mores were regarded by Irish and Norman alike as chieftains. Redivision of the country to satisfy Mortimer, and his arbitrary ejection of the O'Mores, led to war. After suffering defeat in battle against the de Verduns, John de Wogan, who had served his king to the best of his ability, was replaced as justiciar by Sir Edmund Butler.

It must have been at this time that the King of Aileach and those Irish chieftains with whom, for the moment, he was in alliance decided to emulate Bruce in making a stand against England. The controversial remonstrance was probably drawn up as soon as the Scots appeared, although it was not despatched to the pope until the late spring of 1316 at the earliest. Its contents, however, would suggest that it had been some time in preparation, the arrival of Edward Bruce providing necessary inspiration for completion. A sad indictment of English rule, it could not have been sent before 1316, for there was a vacancy in the Papacy after the death, in 1314, of Clement V, the excommunicator of Robert Bruce, who had transferred his seat from the turbulence of Rome to Avignon, then under the protection of Burgundy rather than France.[18] Domhnall Ui Néill, or whoever commissioned the remonstrance, may have remembered the action of the Scottish clergy in 1300, when they 'tendered' the kingdom to Boniface VIII as a papal fief. Perhaps it was thought that the apparent willingness of the Scots to help Ireland would

95

persuade the new pope, whoever he was to be, to take an interest in the land of St Patrick.

The calumnies and the false representations which have been heaped upon us by the English are too well known throughout the world not to have reached the ears of your Holiness [ran the document]. We are persuaded, Most Holy Father, that your intentions are most pure and upright; but from not knowing the Irish except through the misrepresentations of their enemies, your Holiness might be induced to look upon as truth those falsehoods which have been circulated, and to form an opinion contrary to what we merit, which would be to us a great misfortune. It is, therefore, to save our country against such imputations that we have come to the resolution of giving to your Holiness, in this letter, a faithful description and a true and precise idea of the real state at present of our monarchy, if this term can be applied to the sad remains of a kingdom which had groaned so long beneath the tyranny of the kings of England, and that of their ministers and barons, some of whom, though born in our island, continue to exercise over us the same extortions, rapine and cruelties as their ancestors before them have committed. We shall advance nothing but the truth, and we humbly hope that, attentive to its voice, your Holiness will not delay to express your disapprobation against the authors of those crimes and outrages which shall be revealed . . .

The document tells of the plundering of the Irish church by the English, the denial of English justice to Irishmen and the dreadful acts committed against Irishmen by the Norman magnates. Also, it draws the pontiff's attention to the way in which the English king and his predecessors had violated the conditions under which Pope Adrian IV had been 'induced to transfer the sovereignty' of Ireland to Henry II, and how unworthy was that 'impious king' of the confidence shown in him by Adrian. 'Therefore, without the least remorse or conscience, while breath remains, we shall

Ardee, Co. Louth. At the end of the main street can be seen the tower of the castle burned by Edward Bruce in the summer of 1315. (*Irish Tourist Board*)

The motte on the hill at Faughart, Co. Louth, where Edward Bruce met his death. (*Office of Public Works, Dublin*)

attack [the English] in defence of our just rights, and never lay down our arms until we force them to desist . . .'

It is a curious document, to say the least. Lamenting that the Irish were without 'a head to govern them', Domhnall Ui Néill put his name to it not only as King of Aileach but 'lawful heir to the throne of Ireland', that high kingship which had passed out of Ui Néill hands a century before, although in reality on the death of the great Maoil-Seachlainn in 1022. The loss of the throne could hardly be attributed to English skulduggery; rather, as in pre-English days, to the inability of the Ui Néill to stand firm behind a single contestant for the honour, or to defend it against Connacht. Did Domhnall really believe that Ireland had once been a kingdom, the 'sad remains' of which were now cause for lament? Even his most potent ancestors had ruled only in the north, with occasional and brief hegemony over weaker southern states. As far as plundering the church was concerned, it was not an occupation reserved by the English for their peculiar enjoyment.[19] For example, Feidlimidh of Connacht 'plundered and burned the countryside . . . both church and lay property' in 1316, as the *Annals of Clonmacnoise* reported; and the same source shows that, towards the end of the previous century 'the Clan Murtagh burned and ravaged Carbury and attacked its churches'. These were no isolated incidents – monasteries waged war against each other when occasion arose and church property was always seen as fair game. As late as 1402 an anonymous scribe from Co. Longford recorded a war 'without engagement in Muintear Anghaile and churches being plundered', adding what must have been the prayer of generations, 'God help us!'

Certainly the various depredations committed against Irishmen were real and terrible enough and the introduction, first of the alien feudalism, then of King Edward's bureaucracy, had taken toll of the ancient Celtic way of life. Yet the mention of Pope Adrian's Bull is the most curious aspect of the remonstrance: it suggests that the Irish kings accepted the English presence because it had been sanctioned by a pope, and might have been willing to accept it still, had the English kings not violated the Bull. It is this that makes the entire remonstrance suspect, as the Bull now is; especially as no mention was made of the Bull when Henry II arrived in Ireland in 1171.

There is another, equally incredible, passage in the remonstrance: 'In order to attain our object the more speedily and surely, we have invited the gallant Edward Bruce, to whom, being descended from our most noble ancestors, we have transferred, as we justly might, our own right of royal dominion.' This is a repeat of Strongbow's invasion of Leinster with interest, for no Irish king would willingly surrender what he regarded as his inalienable rights to an outsider unless he had no alternative; and when Edward Bruce landed at Larne there was no guarantee that he would be able to subdue or remove the English any more than the Irish leaders had been able to do. It is possible, of course, that Edward, or his brother, had been offered a throne of sorts in the manner that Sitric Silkenbeard, King of Dublin, had offered one to both Sigurd of the Orkneys and the pirate Brodar, tempting them to take arms against his step-father, Brian Boru, in 1014.[20] If it is difficult to see what throne could be given to Sigurd or Brodar had they won the battle at Clontarf, it is harder to imagine what could be offered to the Bruces, unless it was genuinely the high kingship, regarded so tenaciously by the Ui Néill as their own. Unfortunately for Domhnall Ui Néill, Edward Bruce was in need of a throne and, in the light of subsequent events, one cannot but wonder whether the remonstrance was concocted by Bruce himself, without the knowledge of his Irish friends.

Whether it was genuine or not – and the 'original Latin of the memorial' was 'preserved' by John of Fordun, most partisan of the Bruce biographers[21] – it was to take Pope John XXII some time to reply, and then in most unfavourable terms, as will be seen. Poor Domhnall Ui Néill (if, for the moment, we accept him as the author of the remonstrance) put his faith in the wrong pope. John stands out, even in an age of delinquent popes, as one utterly unsuited for the spiritual care of Christendom. Surpassing Boniface VIII in cruelty, he carried out a vicious purge against the reformed Franciscans, whose humble policy of poverty, and the assertion that Christ and his disciples were, like the founder of their own order, mendicants, was anathema to a pleasure-loving prince of the church. John also scandalised Christendom by declaring that none of the saints saw God until the Day of Judgement, a statement that prompted Philip de Valois, King of France, to threaten the pope with the stake.

At the beginning of the invasion, Domhnall's hopes, however vague, seemed justified. Edward Bruce's troops were hardened warriors and in a skirmish shortly after landing easily defeated the followers of the local Norman landowners, Logan, Bisset and Mandeville, who retired to Carrickfergus Castle, built in 1176 and dominated by a square keep, ninety feet high. The castle could not be taken, and indeed remained in English hands while the countryside around was ravaged by Edward. The town, however, was burned, the church being fired while full of terrified townsfolk, an action suited better to a Norse pirate than the chivalrous knight Fordun would have us believe Edward to have been.

Apart from Domhnall, Robert Byset of the Glens and a

handful of lesser chieftains, the countryside was not ready
to flock to Edward's banner, which again makes the veracity
of the remonstrance doubtful. Most of the native chieftains
stood aloof, as 'each wished to retain the chief power over
his own district, and hold it free of tribute and taxation',[22] an
illuminating statement if we believe that Domhnall Ui Néill
was speaking for his peers when offering 'royal dominion'
to Bruce. It is more likely that these chieftains, having so far
resisted utter subjugation by Richard de Burgh, were unwilling to accept it from someone they regarded as another
adventurer who, moreover, was the brother of Richard's
son-in-law.

Edward was certainly an adventurer, although in his day,
and later, the term, if used, did not imply the mercenary of
more recent times. An adventurer was one who engaged
upon a hazardous enterprise, which both the brothers Bruce
had done, although obviously with the intention of gaining
fortune. Both were in a very different league to the adventurers, the real soldiers of fortune, of Elizabethan days.

While Robert's motives in sending his brother to Ulster
have been examined, what of Edward's in leading the expedition? Obviously, while Robert lived, the throne of Scotland was outside his grasp, but to one whose recklessness
before Bannockburn had brought reward, surely this new
adventure could prove even more profitable. Perhaps, with
an inflated opinion of himself, Edward imagined that the
Irish would welcome him with open arms and provide him
with supplies as much as military support. Why else did he
arrive with so few provisions? That provisions were short is
obvious, for as soon as Carrickfergus was burned Edward
discovered the effects of bringing a large army into a country
that, already poorly cultivated, was suffering from years of
internal ravaging. Finding so many of the Irish standing

aloof, he decided to teach them a sharp lesson and his first real battle was against potential allies. 'He plundered the principal part of Uladh,' record the *Annals of Loch Cé*; 'he spoyled all Ulster in Generall, tooke theire hostages ... [and] collected the revenues of that province to himself', according to the Clonmacnoise annalists; and at the Moiry Pass, between Newry and Dundalk, an Irish force, assembled to resist his depredations, was defeated.

Newry was the key to the rich plains of the south, and while Barbour's statement that the odds at the Pass were 'four to one' against Edward, or that 'in that battle was tane or slane all hale the flur of Ullyster', is patently exaggerated – the annalists, usually so ready to detail such holocausts, are silent on the matter – Edward, having gained the Pass, was able to enter the fertile plains of Louth and restock his commissariat.

What, meanwhile, was the reaction from England? What from the administration in Dublin? Edward II was scarcely recovered from Bannockburn and the immediate despatch of an army to confront Bruce was out of the question. At the same time, to ensure England was preoccupied until his brother had established himself in Ireland, Robert Bruce marched across the border towards the end of May. Not until 30th June did King Edward summon a muster, to be ready at Newcastle by the middle of August;[23] but the day before the summons Sir James Douglas entered Co. Durham, marching to Hartlepool, which he occupied while the inhabitants sought refuge on ships anchored in the bay. Douglas spared the town and returned home with much plunder, but for the rest of the year, indeed for several years to come, the north of England was visited regularly by Scottish troops until there could have been little left in the way of plunder, and little for an English army moving northwards.

In Northumberland, for example, the agricultural profits fell by more than four per cent in 1315, by sixteen per cent the following year and by twenty-eight per cent during the summer of 1317, because of Scottish raids.[24] The north became a no man's land, local freebooters taking advantage of the terror caused by the Scots to scavenge the countryside themselves; and when Co. Durham began to pay tribute to Robert, in an attempt to prevent fresh incursions, the freebooters began their own profitable blackmail, in emulation.

Now, too, Robert brought into action what has been regarded as an embryo Scottish navy, although it was more probably a pirate band hiring itself to the king. English records mark the appearance in 1315, and again two years later, of Thomas Don, or Dunn,[25] whose attack on the Isle of Man in February 1315 was followed by the capture of an English ship in Holyhead harbour. The capture does not sound too difficult: the master, and most of the crew, were on shore at the time, but the event shook English morale.

In Ireland, the English were unprepared for the invasion. Levies in the provinces of Munster and Leinster were collected in a hurry[26] and placed under the command of Sir Edmund Butler. Parliament, and heavy borrowing, raised funds just sufficient to meet immediate requirements and the army prepared to march north. Action was too long delayed, for on 29th June Edward Bruce captured the town of Dundalk, pushing a wedge into English territory. The town was ransacked and burned, the leading inhabitants, most of them English burghers, slaughtered, and Edward pressed on into Meath, where Rathmore and Ardee were burned. Ardee was a particular loss to the administration: it was a crucial outpost and the castle, built by Roger Pipard a century earlier and of which the keep today serves as the town courthouse, was an important stronghold rendered useless.

It was not only the alarming progress of Bruce that dismayed the English. Like John de Wogan before him, the justiciar, Butler, had to contend with the ambitions of the Anglo-Irish magnates, and little love was lost between him and Richard de Burgh, who, from his castle at Galway, heard with fury of Scottish depredations on his Ulster estates. In late June or early July, the Red Earl summoned his Connacht tenants to meet him at Roscommon,[27] among them Feidlimidh, the twenty-two-year-old King of Connacht whose elevation to the throne had been accomplished by his foster-father, Maelruanaidh Mac Diarmada, five years earlier. Unfortunately, the young king had little power in the land of his ancestors: de Burgh ruled great tracts of Connacht and dissatisfaction within the royal family had set up the king's kinsman, Ruaidhridhe, as a rival monarch. Feidlimidh was persuaded to join de Burgh at Roscommon by a promise of help against Ruaidhridhe, although subsequent events show that he gave his support in order to weigh up the respective merits of de Burgh and Bruce. This was understandable if one of them might prove the means of regaining his kingdom: Feidlimidh was no less a man of his time than de Burgh or Domhnall Ui Néill.

Richard de Burgh's army 'consisted of twenty cohorts'[28] and marched quickly northwards, making for the territory of the King of Aileach, sparing 'neither spirituall nor Temporall land in every place where they came without respect of saint or shrine or sacred place, from the river of Synan [Shannon] of the south to Cowle-Ryan [Coleraine] of the north . . .' De Burgh intended to make any other northern chieftain think before joining Edward Bruce and also to destroy any sources of supply for the Scottish army. Having passed close to Edward without seeing him,[29] the Red Earl turned south to Ardee, where he suddenly met the justiciar's army – thirty cohorts of well-appointed soldiers 'armed at all points,' said the annalists – coming towards him. Here was a chance for the Scottish expedition to be halted, but de Burgh's dislike of authority lost the English the advantage. The earl saw Bruce's invasion and the 'rebellion' of Domhnall Ui Néill as a personal affair, an intrusion on his territory, and he objected to what he regarded as Butler's interference in the matter. Butler, realising that the countryside, despoiled first by Bruce, now by de Burgh, would not support a third force of troops, withdrew. One wonders whether he hoped that the Scots would rid him of de Burgh before suffering defeat themselves.

Edward Bruce had camped at Faughart, a mile south of the present Irish border and west of the Newry–Dundalk road. A place he was destined to visit again three years later, it was to the Celts a romantic district, associated with the mythical hero, Cuchulain, whose birthplace, Dun Dealgan, from which Dundalk derived its name,[30] was nearby, and with St Brigid, whose birthplace is said to have been in Faughart village. A place of pilgrimage still, it has many shrines dedicated to the saint, one of them containing what is said to be a portion of her skull. More recent research suggests that Brigid was a native of what is today east Co. Cavan and that she was born in Cornasas, in the parish of Kill, the daughter of the head of a school of poetry and his concubine, Brotseach. The mother, apparently, came from the Fothairt, a subject people living in various parts of Ireland, which may account for the association with Faughart. Whatever her origins, she was consecrated a Virgin of Christ on Croghan Breg Ele in Knockbride, Co. Cavan, in AD 439, and with Auxilius was put in charge of the twin monasteries of Knockbride and Corleck, where clergy for the infant church in Ireland were trained.

That the pagan hero, Cuchulain, died in the area, defending Ulster against an invasion from Connacht, was a story that may have come to the attention of Edward Bruce; but he took no chances in the face of this lastest army from the west and retreated northwards, drawing de Burgh into the narrow passes and defiles of Tyrone, ravaging the countryside and breaking down the bridge at Coleraine, over which de Burgh needed to pass. The two armies confronted each other suddenly across the River Bann, although for the moment de Burgh was unable to cross and an exchange of arrows across the river was all either side could accomplish.

At the same time, neither side could sit and wait for the other to take the offensive. Famine was stalking the land and while de Burgh could swallow his pride and sent for reinforcements from Butler, Edward Bruce had no reserves. Instead, he attempted diplomacy: secret negotiations were opened with Feidlimidh of Connacht, promising help in ridding his kingdom of de Burgh and of the rival Ruaidhridhe if the king would now withdraw from the earl's side and return to Connacht. Edward must have painted a picture of a state deprived of much of its fighting force, a state which would soon fall to its rightful king if he pressed home his advantage in de Burgh's absence. Feidlimidh, who had joined de Burgh for similar reasons, weighed the offers in the balance and accepted the Scottish. Richard de Burgh, who could hardly force the king to stay and face Bruce at the same time, watched as the leopard standard of Connacht was carried westward.

Feidlimidh did not then know that Edward was also negotiating with Ruaidhridhe, authorising him to 'war against the English and not to meddle with the lands of

Feidlimidh'. Thus, as Robert Bruce hoped that the Irish expedition would turn English attention away from Scotland, so now Edward hoped that fresh disturbance in Connacht would cause de Burgh to turn homewards. Not only did de Burgh remain where he was; Ruaidhridhe failed to carry out his role as fifth columnist in Connacht as indicated by Edward. 'Hee did not onely warre upon Englishmen, but alsoe upon ffelym [Feidlimidh] and his partakers, and saught all meanes to get the kingdome of Conaught into his own hands',[31] burning Roscommon, Ballintober and other towns; next marching 'incontinently' to Carn-Fraich-mhic-Fidhaigh, the inaugural-place of the Kings of Connacht, where he was invested with the crown. With the exception of the loyal Maelruanaidh Mac Diarmada, Ruaidhridhe received hostages and pledges from the chieftains of Connacht, and, although Feidlimidh soon returned home, it was to be several months before he was able to overthrow his rival and regain the throne.

Richard de Burgh, meanwhile, faced with this defection, had to act quickly. The tale recounted by Barbour maintains that he trapped Edward between the rivers Bann and Foyle and built a dam, hoping to flood the Scottish army. This is disputable,[32] the attempt being also attributed to O'Dempsey, chief of Clanmalier, who, outwardly friendly towards Edward, trapped him between the rivers, having driven away from the neighbourhood all the cattle, so that the Scots had either to drown or to starve to death. Something of the sort may have taken place, although the dramatic appearance of the pirate Thomas Dunn, who sailed up the Bann and ferried the Scots to safety near Coleraine, can be taken as apocryphal. How did Dunn hear of Edward's plight if escape from the river-girt site was impossible? Also, having brought ships sufficient to take away Bruce's army – one imagines the rescue was carried out in a single operation – could he not have provided reinforcements instead? As with so many of the tales attached to the Bruces, it is a good romance but scarcely history.

What did happen was that de Burgh retreated to the town of Connor, four miles south-east of modern Ballymena, Co. Antrim. His forage party was captured by Bruce and the earl's plans to call out the countryside were revealed. This is another Barbour story,[33] however, and it is unlikely that a 'countryside', ravaged and burned as it was, would aid either side. While many local chieftains refused to help Bruce, they had no love for their nominal overlord, de Burgh.

Confrontation came at length on 10th September 1315. Richard de Burgh could not stay inside the walls of Connor indefinitely and perhaps decided that an attack might at least cut a way through the Scots, enabling him to march south for fresh provisions. As he came out of the town, his attention was drawn to the Scottish banners carried in what he presumed was the main body of the army. In fact, Edward was coming up on his rear, the banners having been placed in front of the Scots' baggage train as a feint. The ruse worked, and, as de Burgh attacked, the Scots fell on his rear. The earl escaped with his life, but several of his officers, including his brother, William, were taken prisoner and his army was cut in two, some of the survivors escaping south-east to the invested castle of Carrickfergus, others to Connacht. The Red Earl, lord of Ulster, was a wanderer; 'he remained without force or power in any of the parts of Ireland';[34] his power in Ulster was, momentarily, broken and Connacht was torn between supporters of its rival kings. At the same time 'raigned many Diseases generally throughout the whole kingdome', hardly surprising considering the recent slaughter and destruction. 'Great scarcity of victuals' was followed, according to the chroniclers of Clonmacnoise, by 'ugly and fowle weather' which effectively prevented the only army left unscathed, that of Butler, from taking to the field.

If bad weather and famine kept the English army indoors, they did not prevent Edward from continuing his march of conquest. After sacking Connor, he marched to Carrick-fergus, replenished his stores (although one wonders from where) and sent prisoners and news of his victory to Scotland, at the same time asking his brother for reinforcements. By the early autumn, his nephew, Thomas Randolph, had returned with five hundred men,[35] a number we can reasonably accept, and leaving a guard on the castle he marched south. At Nobber, in Meath, he sacked the town and left a garrison there to forestall any help that might be sent to Carrickfergus.

As no opposition appeared from the south, with the administration undecided as to who should lead it, Edward's confidence increased. For two or three months he was undisturbed, looting and burning Meath at will: a foolish policy in the event of a retreat, but Edward did not contemplate retreat. He was determined to take Dublin.

Early in December he met the first major English attempt to stop him. At Kells, centre of Anglo-Irish rule in Meath, he was confronted by an army led by Roger Mortimer, shortly to replace Butler as justiciar. Mortimer is said to have commanded fifteen thousand men,[36] greatly outnumbering Edward; but to Edward's good fortune the army included a contingent of the de Lacys, whose lands had been divided to accommodate Mortimer in 1308. Had they been able to forget their grievance, their presence in Mortimer's army could have weighed heavily in the English favour. As it was, at the first sign of the Scots pressing home a temporary advantage, the de Lacys went over to Bruce. Mortimer, 'shamefully foiled', retreated to Dublin. Kells, not for the first time, went up in flames.

Edward Bruce was, apparently, invincible. Within three months he had defeated two of the greatest figures in Ireland, and while these victories were due in no small measure to the defection of part of the opposing forces, and by the inability of the English and Anglo-Irish to unite against the common foe, strategy and leadership surely contributed to them. Christmas, 1315, was spent on the shores of Lough Sewdy in Westmeath, and it was a time of more than usual celebration among the Scots. At the end of their first year in Ireland they had suffered no real defeat, no lasting setback. Plunder had been there for the taking in town after town; the campaign had proved easier than winning independence in their own country and, for many of the ordinary troops, far more profitable. The new year offered greater success, not least to Edward himself: if he had ever thought to win Ireland, or to disrupt English rule there, for his brother's sake, he was shortly to satisfy personal ambition and wear a crown.

CHAPTER FIVE

Edward, King of Ireland

The year 1316 was memorable for aspiring kings in Ireland. In Connacht, Feidlimidh, having returned from the north to find his usurping kinsman on the throne, spent the last months of the old year gathering support to regain his crown. None was forthcoming from the Scots, despite the negotiations before the Battle of Connor, and none could be anticipated: Edward Bruce had no interest for now in the fratricidal western kingdom. His deadliest enemy, Richard de Burgh, was a 'wanderer' and the rival Ui Conchobhar princes presented no threat as he marched south towards Dublin.

Initially, Feidlimidh and the 'chiefest men of note that had Recourse to him, Mortagh O'Brien, Prince of Thomond, Mulronye mc Dermott, Prince of Moylurg, Gilbert O'Kelly, Prince of Imania, who were all banished out of their possessions'[1] approached Richard de Burgh for aid; but the earl, who had barely reached Galway Castle alive and had no army, could hardly sympathise with Feidlimidh, whose defection was a cause of his recent defeat by Bruce. The next move was made by Feidlimidh's foster-father, Maelruanaidh Mac Diarmada – Mulronye of the annals – and, at first, seems curious.

110

When [Maelruanaidh] saw soe many exiled noblemen together in one house, hee recomitted with himself, was abashed, and said that he could never be reconed amongst soe many or that number of Deposed chieftains, but would . . . come in favour and credit with Rory [i.e. Ruaidhridhe] and gett his owne againe, which accordingly was don, upon yeelding of Hostages to Rory O'Connor, for keeping his allegiance and fidelity to him . . .[2]

In other words, the loyal Maelruanaidh, who first set Feidlimidh on the throne of his ancestors, went over to the usurper.

While brother might slay brother, cousin slay cousin, such an action as this was contrary to the bonds traditionally forged by fostering, and cannot be taken seriously. Maelruanaidh, probably allowing his foster-son to believe that he had defected, realised that the only way of defeating Ruadhridhe was to ingratiate himself in that quarter, and certainly Ruadhridhe did not refuse the pledges of so eminent a chieftain. Before the end of the year, however, news reached the usurper that 'great exployts' and depredations apparently committed by Feidlimidh were actually the work of Maelruanaidh. Accordingly, Ruadhridhe 'caused to be assembled from all parts his forces' at Ballymote, north of the Boyle near Asslyn. Feidlimidh and his army retreated into the Ox Mountains on the border of Mayo and Sligo, and Ruaidhridhe's anger was vented on towns that had shown support for his rival.

Aughrim, in the territory of Gilbert O'Kelly, was burned, as was Terran in the same principality. Feidlimidh's cause seemed hopeless, when help arrived unexpectedly from the north.

Aodh O'Donnell, ruler of Tir Conaill, was married to a daughter of Magnus O'Conchobhar, *tanaiste*, or heir pre-

111

sumptive, to Feidlimidh under the tanistric system;[3] and, although Tir Conaill and Connacht were frequently at loggerheads, Aodh's wife, Dervorgilla, had a high sense of family loyalty. She summoned a 'great company' of galoglas, descendants of the mercenaries recruited by Donal Oge O'Donnell of Tir Conaill in the previous century, who now formed the élite of her husband's army, and 'gave them a consideration of money' to kill Ruaidhridhe. In short, she placed a price on the usurper's head.

Feidlimidh, meanwhile, was finding new allies in Connacht. In March 1316 he was confident enough to take the field for the last time against his rival, his army being augmented by the troops of Richard de Bermingham, lord of Athenry. It was, to modern eyes at least, an odd association: Richard's father, Sir Piers, had been rewarded by the English administration in 1295 for slaughtering most of the O'Conchobhar princes of Offaly at a Christmas Day banquet, a deed which earned him the title 'hunter out of the Irish'. His family acquired vast estates in the west, eventually becoming Hibernicised as Mac Fheorais,[4] which means the 'son of Piers'. Richard was an opportunist, and his support of Feidlimidh was doubtless motivated by hopes for new gains, rather than by sympathy for the young king or feelings of guilt over his father's massacre of the princes. Probably, he hoped now to eclipse Richard de Burgh: when a great man fell, or was momentarily powerless, there was no shortage of contenders for his place.

At the causeway of Moin-Coinnedha, or Tochar-mona-Coinnedha, 'the causeway of the bog of Coinnidh', in the parish of Templetogher, Co. Galway, the armies of the rivals for the throne of Connacht met. The battle was furious and, at the end of the day, Ruaidhridhe, 'the head of the valour and bravery of the Gaeidhel, and the exterminator of pirates and bandits', according to the chameleon-like annalists of Loch Cé, lay dead upon the field.

Feidlimidh, triumphant, did not hesitate in impressing his success on Connacht. Hostages were taken from recalcitrant chieftains, Ulick O'Ruairc was set up as puppet king of Breifne, a vassal-state of Connacht with aspirations to independence,[5] and from 'the place called Castle Corran' to Roua (now the Robe, flowing into the eastern side of Lough Mask) the countryside was burned. Feidlimidh tasted real power for the first time: marching into Munster, he received pledges from Muircheartach O'Brien, King of Thomond and a descendant of Brian Boru, whose kingdom had once been part of Connacht,[6] and returned with him to Roscommon, where a castle owned by Richard de Burgh was burned. Feidlimidh could have posed a major problem for the English, indeed for Edward Bruce, had he not turned against those Anglo-Normans who helped him regain his throne. At Athlone he slew as many of the 'foreigners' as could be found, many of them de Burgh and de Bermingham tenants.

Although Richard de Burgh appears still to have been powerless, in the summer of 1316 his brother, William, captured by Bruce at Connor and sent as a prisoner to Scotland, returned to Connacht. One can imagine his release being negotiated by his niece, Queen Elisabeth, but, however it was brought about, William de Burgh had the energy necessary to rally the 'foreigners' of Connacht. On the Feast of St Lawrence, 10th August, the battle for supremacy in the west was fought near Athenry. On Feidlimidh's side was an impressive gathering of Celtic Ireland: Donnchadh O'Brien, recently crowned King of Thomond, Ulick O'Ruairc of Breifne, Tadhg O'Cellaigh of Ui Maine in Galway and O'Maoil-Seachlainn, who, despite the presence of de Lacys, de Verduns and Roger Mortimer, maintained tenaciously the title King of Meath. With William de Burgh were Richard de Bermingham, lately Feidlimidh's ally, and those described by the *Annals of Ulster* as the 'Foreigners of the greater part of the Half of Conn'.[7]

Bearing in mind the King of Connacht's recent whirlwind success, and notwithstanding the annalists' claim regarding the foreigners, the advantage surely lay with Feidlimidh. Richard de Burgh, who was not present at the battle, was still rebuilding his own scattered forces, and, unless William had returned with a considerable number of released companions, the outcome of the battle was due to good fortune rather than numerical superiority.

Perhaps the Irish lost heart when Feidlimidh fell beneath the leopard standard.[8] Others who lost their lives that day included Tadhg O'Cellaigh, Diarmaid Mac Diarmada, *tanaiste* to the loyal prince of Moylurg, and so great a collection of men of royal blood that most of the chroniclers commented that never before had so many 'sons of kings and of chiefs' been slain in one battle. Also a victim was Magnus, *tanaiste* of Connacht, whose daughter had raised the galoglas in aid of Feidlimidh – Dervorgilla herself died before the end of the year, perhaps of distress at the end of her family's aspirations. The survivors inaugurated another Ruaidhridhe as King of Connacht, but any hope of independence for the kingdom died with Feidlimidh. An unintentional memorial to that hope was erected by the victors in the shape of new walls for Athenry, paid for by the sale of arms and goods taken from the bodies of Feidlimidh's army, a vivid illustration of the dead king's support. Ironically, that support served only to increase the power of the foreigners, notably the de Berminghams.

What of Edward Bruce, who must have observed events in Connacht with delight, as they preoccupied his potential foes? After celebrating Christmas on the edge of Lough Sewdy, he continued to lay waste the country in the middle of Ireland and in Leinster. English burghers in Dublin trembled at the thought of his advance, but, with the administration concerned more with petty quarrels than with a plan of campaign to defeat Bruce, the burghers were offered scant protection, and more than one of them must have retreated across St George's Channel. While Mortimer, now justiciar, attempted to reorganise an army, Edward continued his irresistible progress and unless aid came from England, which was unlikely with the king and his cousin, Thomas of Lancaster, in open opposition, there was nothing to halt him.

In the event it was that inevitable side-effect of war, famine, which stayed Bruce's march on Dublin. The constant rape of the countryside, combined with unusually wet summers in 1315 and 1316, brought Ireland to starvation; and England, which had also experienced a cycle of wet seasons, fared little better. The annalists saw the calamity as being 'the hand of God outstretched to punish sin', as they invariably explained great national disasters, which brought small comfort to those who saw the price of corn quadruple in twelve months. The famine of 1316 was the start of a succession of 'fearful visitations'[9] that made the fourteenth century one of misery on both sides of the Channel – with the Black Death of 1348 being the most awful, but not the last, of calamities attributed to heavenly vengeance. The chroniclers recorded the deaths only of eminent people, the mortality rate among ordinary folk being of little interest, although more terrible.

Much of the famine, of course, had been caused by Edward Bruce as he marched south, burning the crops and laying waste the land on either side. By the end of March

1316 he was faced with the alternatives of besieging Dublin or retreating to Ulster to replenish his stores and, if possible, to take the castle of Carrickfergus, still holding out as the last English outpost in the north-east. Dublin was isolated and, had Bruce appeared, would probably have surrendered. But Carrickfergus presented another danger: if, unlikely as it seemed at the time, the English king sent reinforcements, they could relieve the castle and march on Edward's rear. He decided to return to Ulster and settle with Carrickfergus, an obvious mistake if we believe that Dublin would have fallen easily. At the same time, to hold Dublin, Edward would require more troops from Ulster: could he risk gaining Dublin only to lose Carrickfergus? He knew that the allegiance of Irish chieftains was swift to change, besides which many of the Ulster chieftains had not supported him in the first place. Whether or not he threw away his one chance of success, as has been alleged,[10] by returning north is a debatable point. Did he have a clear chance of success, a chance to crush the English in Ireland as effectively as they were crushed at Bannockburn? As he made his decision, the Battle of Athenry was four months in the future and Connacht, base of the most powerful Anglo-Norman magnates, was crippled with internecine strife. Did, perhaps, Edward believe that Feidlimidh could win and hold Connacht and, having done so, allow the Scots free passage through the rest of the island?

In Scotland, with the English threat removed, Robert Bruce gradually gained support among the nobles and more quickly among the ordinary people, and he did not face a situation in which Celtic kings were competing with him for supremacy. In Ireland, despite the mutual antipathy of the de Burghs and the O'Conchobhar princes for the English administration, and despite the transmogrification of the

Norman de Bermingham into Mac Fheorais, or even de Burgh into Burke, there were in Bruce's day two distinct races contesting hegemony, not simply of the whole island but of individual states therein. Robert's principal enemy was England; Edward Bruce faced Celt and Anglo-Irish, as well as the officialdom represented now by Mortimer. He needed to subdue or seduce all before his invasion could be regarded as a success, before his position neared that of his brother in Scotland.

Eventually the ultimate victor in Connacht would confront him, and, while the capture of Dublin would increase his power dramatically, his Achilles' heel remained Carrick-fergus.

Thus Edward returned to Ulster, marching through Kildare and Leix and burning the church at Abbeyleix – 'Leys in Lagenia' or Leinster – and taking what was probably the castle of Moy Cova at Iveagh, Co. Down,[11] a lucky omen with Carrickfergus in mind. The church belonged to the de Vesci family, who were an early example of Hibernicisation, which is probably why it suffered. Another of the 'Old English' to fall foul of Edward was Lord Logan, a member of the family planted in Ulster by King John and whose kinsmen had taken refuge in Carrickfergus Castle in May 1315. A somewhat biased account of Bruce's expedition[12] suggests that Logan, who was sentenced to death and executed by 'one of Bruce's courts of justice', had supported, then deserted, the Scots, 'for Edward Bruce, in humanity, would hardly have put a prisoner of war to death'. That is no reason for supposing Logan to have changed sides: both Edward and Robert Bruce were humane when it suited them, and the murder of John Comyn was hardly an example of humanity. Yet so contradictory were the mores of the age that a story told by Barbour of Robert halting a march until 'a poor laundress' had given birth may be genuine. Lord Logan may have been a hostage against the surrender of Carrickfergus, executed as a summary warning to the garrison. The taking of the castle could not be treated as the taking of Stirling, with a chivalrous breathing-space.

The defence of Carrickfergus was commanded by Sir Thomas Mandeville, a kinsman of Roger, one of the lesser claimants of 1291. During Edward's absence in the midlands, Mandeville had sent his brothers to the Isle of Man, where fresh provisions were gathered and a message for help sent to the English fleet.[13] The fleet was presumably that led by Sir John de Athy, afterwards constable of Carrickfergus, who shortly after the Battle of Connor had captured and beheaded the pirate, Thomas Dunn. This would at least explain how the Mandevilles were able to reach Man in safety. On 10th April fifteen ships arrived at Carrickfergus, the newcomers joined the garrison and a force now left the castle to take Bruce by surprise.

How it was that Edward was unprepared for the attack, or that he was unaware of the arrival of the ships until it was too late, is a mystery. Barbour maintains that Edward had arranged a truce during the Easter celebrations:

> In time of truce issued they [the garrison]
> On such a time as Easter day,
> When God rose all mankind to win
> From tarnish of old Adam's sin,

which, if true, adds immediately to the prestige of Edward Bruce. Here, again, was that chivalrous knight who would not consider spilling the blood of his fellow men at a holy time of year. A more likely story is that Edward's troops, exhausted and resting after their march through a famine-haunted land, failed to see the ships coming in under cover of dark. An attempt by Robert Bruce to take Berwick in January of the same year failed because bright moonlight gave away the position of his ships. Edward was caught off guard, an admission not tolerated by his eulogists, and it was only after hard fighting that Mandeville was driven back into the castle. Once more the gates were shut in Edward's face, once more the garrison sat down to await help from England.

England did nothing. Edward II and Thomas of Lancaster were feuding, with Thomas holding mock court in considerable state in the north and ignoring the king's authority, while the king amused himself with 'a great company of simple people' in the south. After Bannockburn, Thomas had become all-powerful, maintaining that his cousin's defeat had been the penalty for refuting the decrees of the Lords Ordainers, a committee of noblemen established in 1310 to reform the royal household and government and thus to curtail the king's power and remove his favourites.[14] The king had prevaricated until the beginning of 1312, accepting some of the ordinances, including what turned out to be the temporary banishment of Gaveston, but now civil war seemed inevitable. In May 1312 Gaveston (whom, it is interesting to note, was termed 'a very noble knight' in the *Annals of Loch Cé*) surrendered to the barons besieging him in Scarborough Castle. His real faults seem to have been an unfortunate sense of humour and a wit which irritated the barons, coupled with the fact that he was a foreigner in an England that was becoming increasingly nationalistic. Gaveston was killed at Blacklow Hill, near Warwick, and a reconciliation between king and barons did not take place until the winter of 1313, when Thomas and others apologised publicly for encompassing the Gascon's death, in

119

return receiving full pardons and a promise that their alleged grievances would be investigated. The king could really do nothing else.

Lancaster, however, was determined to humiliate the king. His chance came when writs of summons for military service in Scotland were sent out. He refused to attend in person, claiming that the ordinances did not permit the king to make war without the permission of the Lords Ordainers and, consequently, he was not at Bannockburn. King Edward returned home, his person and his country in a parlous state: Lancaster refused to have anything to do with him and occupied his time in private warfare against anyone foolhardy enough to oppose him in the north. His example was mimicked by the lesser nobility and gentry in that part of England, the lack of law and authority encouraging family vendettas. One such broke out between Sir Geoffrey de Chadderton and Adam de Oldham, both Lancashire men of old family, with Sir Geoffrey a staunch adherent of Thomas. In Adam's lukewarm acceptance of the local status quo, Sir Geoffrey saw the chance to settle a long-standing personal feud, and hostilities between the two continued until 1322, in which year the king finally took action against his cousin, marching north, scattering the rebel forces and executing their leader.

This, however, was some time in the future, and in 1315, when Sir Geoffrey began his campaign of partisan fervour against Adam de Oldham, Thomas of Lancaster had no fear of sudden action on the part of his king. So much was he an egoist, so tyrannical his rule, that even his wife deserted him; and in 1315 he was powerful enough to dismiss the royal chancellor and treasurer and replace them with Lancastrian puppets.

It is also worth noting that, during Scottish raids south of the border, Thomas's estates were, generally, bypassed, and rumours spread that the earl was, if not in league with Bruce, at least ignoring his incursions. With or without his tacit support, Bruce was able to levy tribute on Durham and Northumberland without opposition; and if news of this reached Carrickfergus the beleaguered occupants at the castle surely despaired of help.

Even so, Edward Bruce was aware that the English king and barons had been reconciled several times in the past, and if he waited for Carrickfergus to be starved into submission he risked losing gains already made in the midlands of Ireland. Already, Richard de Burgh was recovering his strength and several Irish chieftains, hitherto aloof, now joined the English in Dublin. Among them was the King of Leinster, Donal O'Caomhanach, or Kavanagh, a descendant of the Ui Cennselach dynasty which had ruled Leinster until the Normans came. The English, although they did not recognise his title, bought his services with a half-yearly payment from the Exchequer;[15] and, with Connacht again in a semblance of order, Edward could not afford to sit outside Carrickfergus while other chieftains followed Kavanagh's example.

The position was indeed becoming desperate and in May Edward decided to emulate his brother's action in 1306 and declare himself king, perhaps to rally fresh support from the Celts, perhaps to show the English and those who procrastinated that he meant business. Not least, if we believe Fordun, his ambition to rank equally with Robert would be realised.

On 2nd May 1316, having withdrawn to Dundalk, he was crowned on the hill of Dun Dealgan, or Maoldun, the 'bare or bald hill or fort',[16] a mile west of the town and, traditionally, the birthplace of the hero Cuchulain. An eighteenth-century antiquarian has described it thus:[17]

A very remarkable mount, situated upon an eminence . . . and a bold point of view about the bay and a great part of the country round about. The mount, or chief guard, appears to be all artificial, and is surrounded with a magnificent ditch. The height of the terraswork in the middle, from the plane of the trench, is in some place 50 feet, and the circumference of the top is upwards of 460 feet. Upon the east and west side of it are two other forts adjoining to the outward ballum of the ditch . . . which, together with the main mount, cover all the summit of the hill upon which they stand, and for several miles, to the north and south, make a very formidable and grand appearance . . .

By the end of the eighteenth century the site had been decorated with a folly, erected on the highest point by a local landowner, Patrick Byrne of Castletown; and a driveway was made through the mound in a half-circle from the north-east. The 'formidable and grand appearance' of this pre-Celtic fortress remains, however, and it is not difficult to imagine the scene enacted there on that spring day of six centuries ago. There is no doubt that Edward, with a keen sense of the dramatic, selected Dun Dealgan for his coronation on purpose. In his day it was still one of the most celebrated places in the island and, although, like the hill of Tara in Meath, long deserted, the associations of Cuchulain and his 'house, white on the outside, and visible from afar to mariners sailing on the sea of Muir nIocht'[18] were remembered wherever the *seanchais*, or storytellers of the Celts, assembled.

Not all historians accept 2nd May 1316 as the date of the coronation. It has been suggested that Edward declared himself king after defeating Roger Mortimer at Kells in

December 1315, while an anonymous manuscript[19] claims that he was crowned long before the battle. The *Annals of Loch Cé* and the *Annals of Clonmacnoise*, relying on earlier accounts, state merely that he was 'proclaimed king' or 'given the name of king' without offering a date but suggesting it was shortly after he arrived in Ireland. The compilers of the *Annals of Ulster*, regarded generally as the most reliable of the chroniclers, ignored the event altogether, referring to Bruce by his name throughout and treating his invasion as an irritating departure from the succession of more usual internal disruptions.

Of course, Edward might style himself king from the day of his arrival and postpone his coronation until the opportune moment. Certainly, after the Battle of Kells would have been a suitable time and Christmas, being imminent, would have given additional significance to the occasion, which is why the annalists would surely have noted it. But Edward was not at Dun Dealgan for Christmas and Carrickfergus was still in enemy hands. That the castle did not fall or surrender in the following spring, and the fact that de Burgh and the English were rebuilding their forces, suggests that Edward brought forward a coronation he had intended should take place when the last English outpost in the north was in his hands. Carrickfergus, isolated, had scant means of knowing what was taking place elsewhere in the island; and the news of their besieger's coronation might convince them that the country was his, and further resistance was useless. Psychological warfare was not a product of later centuries.

The stories of Edward becoming king long before May 1316 have been encouraged by the wording of the remonstrance sent to Pope John XXII. The document has already been called into question, but *something* was sent to Avignon, although no answer was received for several months, and then to the discomfiture of the Irish who had supposedly written it. John XXII does not seem to have been overfond of replying to letters from the west: although he eventually recognised Robert as King of Scotland, the Declaration of Arbroath, sent to him by the Scottish nobility in 1320, asking for acknowledgement of the king, was not answered for eight years.

The ceremony at Dun Dealgan increased Edward Bruce's morale. If the Irish princes with him doubted the legality of the move, they said nothing. That they received him with open arms as their sovereign is debatable, as is the suggestion[20] that his success in the midlands had been the signal for Feidlimidh and lesser princes to plunder the Anglo-Irish or English elsewhere. It is unquestionable that Edward's victories enabled dissatisfied Celts or power-hungry Normans to assault their neighbours without fear of retribution from a beleaguered Dublin, although the risk of that was usually small; but as for the Irish receiving him rapturously as *Ardri*, such an idea can be disproved from the time he landed at Olderfleet.

It is also difficult to know how seriously to take the claim that Welsh princes sent a deputation to Edward, asking for help against the English in their country.[21] The final subjugation of Wales by Edward I of England in 1283, and the proclamation the next year of the future Edward II as Prince of Wales, had been followed by periodic insurrections; but it was not until 1400 that Owain Glyndwr, a descendant of the last native prince, Llewellyn ap Griffith, launched the greatest and final attempt to evict the English. The Welsh aristocracy was as disunited as the Irish, and although it had combined in 1164 to resist, unsuccessfully, the invasion of Henry II, regional feuds continued. Like Ireland, Wales had never been one country, although from time to time the Kings of Gwynedd, or north Wales, had been recognised as *pendragon*, the equivalent of *Ardri* or the Saxon *bretwalda*, by the states of Powys, Dyfed and Brycheiniog.

Any deputation sent to Edward Bruce may have come from a solitary chieftain who saw the chance to extend his territory and who had been impressed by the misfortune inflicted on the English in Scotland and Ireland. Edward's reaction, we are told,[22] was 'arrogant in the extreme': he demanded absolute power in Wales – recognition as *pendragon*, in other words – and the Welsh, who had suffered already from Roger Mortimer and other Marcher lords, did not pursue their negotiations.

For the moment, Bruce was concentrating on that Achilles' heel at Carrickfergus, and immediately after his coronation returned to the castle and demanded its surrender. The defenders, who can be compared with the people of Drogheda and Londonderry three centuries later, continued to hold out. One chronicler[23] maintains that on 24th June Mandeville agreed to consider terms, and a deputation of thirty Scotsmen entered the castle, only to find the gates locked behind them and the siege continued. If the garrison hoped to find hostages among the deputation, it was to be disappointed. For a year the castle had defied Edward, but, apart from the brief and bold foray to the Isle of Man, the defenders had been unable to take in fresh provisions. The situation deteriorated daily, cattle hides being the staple diet – with, according to one tradition, eight of the thirty captured Scotsmen augmenting it.[24] Still England made no move to help a garrison whose loyalty had been so manifestly proven.

At length, the administration in Dublin decided to act. In July, eight ships were stocked in Drogheda, still in English hands, and despatched along the coast. With the bulk of Edward's army encamped before Carrickfergus and, presumably, the ships he had brought to Ireland still in the harbour, the little fleet was a forlorn hope, and it never received the chance to lift the siege or to give new hope to the besieged. Richard de Burgh, Earl of Ulster, was negotiating with his son-in-law, Robert Bruce, for the return of his son, or sons, captured at the Battle of Connor and sent to Scotland with their uncle, William. A prolonged siege could jeopardise their early release and, as the ships left Drogheda, de Burgh intercepted them and turned them back. The garrison at Carrickfergus, much of it made up of de Burgh's tenants, had been sacrificed.

The castle held out until September. Only then was it admitted that further resistance was useless, as the dead and dying piled up in the courtyards, as the stench became unbearable and as it was made clear that England and de Burgh had abandoned the defenders. Barbour tells us that Edward Bruce granted the gallant people their lives: what was the point in taking vengeance on pitiful skeletons now that the fortress was his?

In Dublin, Roger Mortimer panicked. Besides offering a reward of one hundred pounds for the capture of Bruce, and ordering each Englishman or loyalist to be responsible for the protection of his own lands (a potent indication of the administration's inability to protect its own), nothing else was done in the way of defence. In the end, it was left to the merchants and townspeople to prepare to withstand the Scots.

It was about this time that an answer to the remonstrance arrived from Avignon. As far as Domhnall Ui Néill was concerned, the reply was equivocal.[25] The pope wrote direct to Edward II, pointing out that neither he nor his prede-

cessors, including Henry II, had paid any attention to the
object of Pope Adrian's Bull, but had, 'passing the bounds
that had been prescribed to them, heaped upon the Irish
the most unheard of miseries and persecution, and had,
during a long period, imposed on them a yoke of slavery
which could not be borne . . .' He suggested 'urgent reforms',
in case 'it might be too late hereafter to apply a remedy, when
the spirit of revolt had grown stronger'. At the same time,
however, he condemned the invasion and excommunicated
Edward Bruce and he threatened his supporters, among
whom Domhnall Ui Néill was numbered, with a similar
interdict. How the threat was received by the Ui Néill is
unknown – their annalists ignored it – but it may have
contributed to the deposition of Domhnall less than two
years later. Also, it is not insignificant that, when the final
battle in the saga of Edward Bruce was fought, none of the
Ui Néill are recorded as being in the Scottish ranks or dying
on the field.

Edward Bruce was unperturbed by the sentence of excommunication. His brother, whom the pope insisted on ad-
dressing as 'the lord Robert, acting as king of Scots', rather
than as King of Scotland, had been excommunicated for a
decade but had the support of the Scottish church. One of
the indictments against English rule in Ireland had been the
maltreatment of the native clergy and monasteries, and
while Bruce burned churches with no less enthusiasm than
his contemporaries he may have considered the idea of
posing, in due course, as saviour of the Irish church and
restorer of its ancient liberties, thereby gaining its favour.
Robert and Edward Bruce were more aware of the worldly
aspirations of the church, a church militant indeed, and of
the undignified pretensions of the Papacy than were the
lesser princes of Ulster. Remote in their glens and on their

mountainsides, they were cut off from the mainstream of world affairs and retained a simple, if frequently misplaced, faith in their spiritual head, be he in Rome or Avignon.

On the English, the papal reply had no effect. They were not under threat of excommunication and they had already indicated, when Scotland appealed for help to a previous pontiff in 1300, that interference in English politics was not to be tolerated. In any case, with no real leader in England, there was little chance that the papal comments would be either rejected or implemented; and after the surrender of Carrickfergus there was the real possibility that the days of English rule in Ireland, or at least English officialdom in Dublin, were numbered.

It was Robert Bruce who next turned his attention to Ireland. In March 1316 his nephew, Sir Thomas Randolph, had returned to Scotland for reinforcements and, according to several sources, a request from Edward for his brother to join him in Ireland. How genuine this request was, and whether it was ever made, is difficult to assess. Having been successful on his own, and bearing in mind his irritation over his position as a younger brother, it is hard to imagine Edward wanting Robert at his side. If he had ever promised to win Ireland for Robert, or to destroy English power there so that Scotland would be secure from that quarter, he had in the meantime fulfilled another ambition on the hill of Dun Dealgan. Edward Bruce was King of Ireland, an equal of the King of Scotland, and had made himself so in a quarter of the time it had taken Robert to consolidate his position.

Was Robert willing to acquiesce to his brother's ambition? With Scotland for the moment at peace, he could leave the administration in the capable hands of Sir James Douglas and his son-in-law, Walter the High Steward, and investigate personally events across the water. If he did mistrust Edward, he showed no signs of it, at least when in Ireland, but he surely harboured doubts over his brother's coronation. The Irish expedition, as it happened, had been relatively worthless from the point of view of preoccupying England. Famine, northern raids and the disunity of the royal family and barons had been occupation enough for the enemy. Edward II or Thomas of Lancaster, or whoever imagined they ruled England, had left Dublin to face the perils of the invasion alone, and while England was in disarray Scotland had nothing to fear from men like Richard de Burgh, who would only consider invading Scotland if paid to do so. King Robert may have gained his throne with his brother's help, but he held it now with the support of Douglas and Thomas Randolph's father, the Earl of Moray. Reckless Edward was much safer out of Scotland, yet twice he had called for reinforcements and if Scotland was to maintain her independence, particularly against the time of England's recovery, Scotsmen could ill be spared to fight abroad.

It is feasible to assume that Robert considered negotiating an alliance with the Ulster princes, for a permanent foothold in Ireland would be a permanent distraction for the English. However, if Edward Bruce insisted on a crown and a kingdom of his own, and one larger than north-east Ulster, problems could arise. A Scottish expeditionary force in Ireland indefinitely was out of the question, while reduced English authority and a stronger Scottish presence depended on the support of the native chieftains, so fluctuating in their allegiances. Still less confidence could be placed in the Anglo-Irish such as the de Lacys, who, having deserted Mortimer at Kells, were now declaring their support for the English crown.[26] Robert's decision to visit Ireland was not so much the answer to a fraternal request as an opportunity to see the situation for himself, and to discover at first hand exactly what had been achieved by the island's self-styled king.

CHAPTER SIX

Many Galoglas

The strength of the reinforcements arriving at Carrickfergus with Robert Bruce some time late in 1316, indeed of the army they came to support, is unknown. It has been computed,[1] without reliable evidence, that the united force stood at twenty thousand, an absurdly high figure and one little smaller than that 'greatest army England had ever sent forth' to Bannockburn, three years earlier. The annalists record simply that Robert arrived, 'along with many galoglas', to help with the expulsion of the 'Foreigners from Ireland';[2] and we can believe that he brought with him a band of those iron-helmeted foot-soldiers, armed with long sword and broad axe. If Robert intended his visit to be brief and decisive, he could have chosen no better men to accompany him.

As we have seen, a Scottish expeditionary force could not remain in Ireland indefinitely. Early in February, the brothers marched south, through Saul, associated with St Patrick, to Downpatrick, once the headquarters of John de Courcy, where the Benedictine abbey founded by him was sacked and burned. The Bruces could not leave potential succour for an encircling movement from de Burgh, although surely they were also cutting off provisions needed

131

EDWARD BRUCE

by themselves in case of a sudden retreat. Sir John Froissart,[3] writing his celebrated, and still highly readable, *Chronicles of England, France and Spain* at the end of the fourteenth century, offers a vivid picture of a Scottish army on the march:

The Scots are bold, hardy and much inured to war. When they make their invasions . . . they march from twenty to four-and-twenty leagues without halting, as well by night as day; for they are all on horseback, except the camp followers, who are on foot. The knights and esquires are well mounted on large bay horses, the common people on little galloways. They bring no carriages with them . . . neither do they carry with them any provisions of bread and wine; for their habits of sobriety are such, in time of war, that they will live for a long time on flesh half sodden, without bread, and drink the river-water without wine . . . they dress the flesh of their cattle in the skins, after they have taken them off; and, being sure to find plenty of them in the country which they invade, they carry none with them. Under the flaps of his saddle, each man carries a broad plate of metal; behind the saddle, a little bag of oatmeal: when they have eaten too much of the sodden flesh, and their stomach appears weak and empty, they place this plate over the fire, mix with water their oatmeal, and when the plate is heated, they put a little of the paste upon it, and make a thin cake, like a cracknel or biscuit, which they eat to warm their stomachs: it is therefore no wonder, that they perform a longer day's march than other soldiers . . .

In a land racked by famine, the oatmeal cakes must have formed the staple, if not the only, diet of the army. Of course, Dublin, with its direct sea link to England, would be well provisioned, but the Bruces now had to gamble on its surrender. Oatmeal was not limitless.

So fast was the southward march that neither side seemed aware of the other's movements. On 16th February the brothers reached Slane in Co. Meath 'without being perceived',[4] an indication that their army was nowhere near the twenty thousand men suggested. Even in a land despoiled, it would hardly have escaped observation, its presence un- reported to de Burgh, who, that month, was staying at his manor of Ratoath, in a direct line between Slane and Dublin. It is unlikely that the Bruces realised de Burgh was so close, for they marched into an ambush: de Burgh allowed them to pass through an unidentified defile and attacked the rear, hoping to 'draw them back to their destruction'.[5] But Robert, we are told, saw the trap and saved the day; more likely, de Burgh's force was smaller than the Scots' and despite the eulogistic verses on the 'battle', in which

> In all the war of Ireland
> So hard a fight was not seen,[6]

de Burgh decided to retire to Dublin.

Neither side reckoned with the growing impatience of the citizens of Dublin. With Mortimer and de Burgh unable to stem the Scottish tide, the merchants and burghers of the city, many of them English and all with their livelihoods at risk, took action themselves. To those solid tradesmen de Burgh had always presented a cavalier attitude; further- more, his connection by marriage with the Bruces was well known, and who could tell what secret negotiations he might undertake if his own power was threatened? He may have run from Bruce now, but if his dealings with the native rulers in Connacht were reliable indicators of his character, what was to prevent him, for the sake of his estates, opening the city gates to his son-in-law? Action was swift: led by their mayor, Robert Nottingham, a band of citizens went to de Burgh's lodgings in St Mary's Abbey, a Cistercian house standing north of the River Liffey until dissolution in the sixteenth century, and largely rebuilt in 1304 after one of the disastrous fires that swept medieval Dublin. There, the

133

mayor placed de Burgh under arrest and took him to Dublin Castle.

The news spread quickly. The ordinary people of Dublin had no love for the Red Earl and, the same night, Monday, 18th February,[7] a mob attacked the castle and tried to storm de Burgh's quarters. Eleven of his servants are said to have been killed and two days later St Mary's Abbey was ransacked, presumably in retaliation for the monks giving shelter to the earl.

Richard de Burgh, lord of Ulster and Connacht, was for the time being powerless to act, and the burghers now took steps to defend the city. The council decided that should the Scots present a major threat – and, it must be remembered, no one seemed to know the size of the army – the suburbs must be burned, notably the western area around St Thomas's Abbey, now Thomas Street, leading from the direction of the castle to St James's Gate.[8] St Saviour's, north of the river, was to be demolished, the stones to be used to extend the city wall and protect the quay. The bridge across the Liffey, for long referred to as the Old Bridge, built in 1210 on the site of the present Father Mathew Bridge[9] and, apparently, the only bridge into the city until 1670, was to be broken down.

Much was at stake. If the Bruces captured Dublin what remained of the English administration in Ireland would collapse, and with it would go the fortunes, businesses and homes of many honest citizens, worthy successors to the Vikings, who had built up the city on a sound basis of commerce. If the threat passed, there would be time enough to deal with the wrath of the Red Earl, who had proved powerless to protect the leading mercantile community of the island.

The news was not heartening: Robert and Edward Bruce

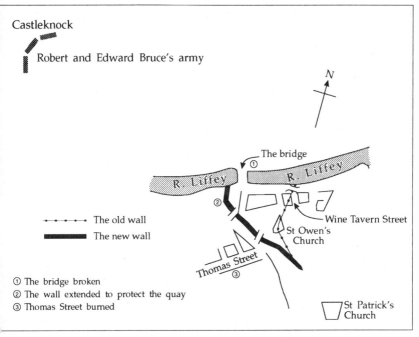

Defensive measures taken to protect Dublin when the Bruces
arrived at Castleknock in 1317

arrived at Castleknock, to the north-west of the city walls, and Robert Nottingham made the decision which saved Dublin. The wooden buildings in Thomas Street were fired, the bridge was broken down, and cattle and other provisions were brought in quickly from the immediate district. But the expected siege never came: the Bruces withdrew from Castleknock without striking a blow at the hastily repaired city walls. The cost was high – an estimated ten thousand pounds in damage,[10] although much of it was caused by the looting Dublin mob and the destruction, deliberate or otherwise, of two city churches, the Magdalen Chapel and St John's, besides countless private and business premises. Yet the initiative of Robert Nottingham and his fellow councillors was appreciated in at least one quarter, ironically that

135

from which they might have expected help. The following year, Edward II granted his pardon to the 'Dublin commonalty' for having burned the suburbs and for taking provisions from men living near the city.

Why did Robert and Edward Bruce turn back? The suggestion that they had no siege-train with which to tackle Dublin[11] we can assume to be correct, especially after Froissart's account of a marching Scots army.

It is equally certain that Robert knew he could not risk a protracted siege of a city that had recently provisioned itself, and that delay could attract support from Mortimer and levies raised in Munster and southern Leinster. There was no time to wait for ships to come down from Carrickfergus; indeed, it was essential to retreat there before an English blockade of the northern port could be put into effect.

Robert cannot have failed to realise that his brother's expedition was little more than an adventure in self-aggrandisement and that any hopes he may have entertained of a united Celtic empire were far from being realised. Robert had won his own kingdom and had managed to hold it, but only to a considerable extent through the loyalty of men such as Douglas and Randolph. In Ireland, it seemed, there was no such loyalty among his peers.

To Robert, now, the removal of the English from Berwick was of greater importance than the sack of Dublin, which, it was only too apparent, would prove difficult. His route back to Carrickfergus, or at least the route he is said to have followed,[12] was curious. Leaving Castleknock on the Feast of St Matthias, 24th February, he is supposed to have spent six weeks on the journey, marching first southwards to Naas and then turning south-west to Limerick, laying waste as he passed through the estates of the former justiciar, Sir Edmund Butler. At Naas he is said to have been joined by the de Lacys,[13] the clan whose desertion of Mortimer at Kells in December 1315 had given Edward Bruce a considerable victory and who now, presumably, withdrew their recent allegiance to Edward II. Naas went up in flames, followed by Castledermot, Gowran and Callan, which was reached on 12th March, the Bruces then turning to Limerick –'the southernmost city that in Ireland may be found,' said Barbour – which proved impregnable. The army then marched eastwards, through the midlands, arriving at Trim, north-west of Dublin, shortly after Easter, leaving a trail of destruction in its wake.

Can we believe that, having left Dublin in February without attempting to storm the city, Robert Bruce, an experienced general, marched what was little more than an expeditionary force, with or without de Lacy support, into unknown territory; or that he risked an engagement with the justiciar's army? Can we believe that he hoped to capture Limerick, having been wise enough to admit the futility of besieging Dublin? Edward Bruce might well have called for a trail of fire to be taken into Munster, but would his brother, anxious to reach Carrickfergus and the security of his ships, have agreed to so roundabout a journey, especially as supplies, oatmeal notwithstanding, were running low? Certainly, the de Lacys, if they now sided with the Scots in order to irritate their common enemy Mortimer, could indulge in a foraging expedition, or simply a trail of plunder with their momentary support of Bruce an excuse; and Trim could well have suffered a visitation from the Scots, a lightning raid to seize supplies. Then the march north would begin, as quickly and as lightly provisioned as possible if it was to be accomplished in no longer time than the downward journey. The Bruces had left Carrickfergus in early February and, taking into consideration halts for the sacking of Downpatrick and elsewhere, they had reached Castleknock by 18th February. They could not afford to take six weeks to return.

The march via Limerick could well have been made by the de Lacys, to divert attention from the Bruces: that the brothers went that way becomes even less plausible when we learn that Barbour, never weary of eulogising Robert Bruce, brings the Scots face to face with an army of forty thousand men, led by de Burgh. The earl was still imprisoned in Dublin Castle, although an unidentified source, mentioned by Haverty, would have the leaders as Richard de Clare, Thomas FitzGerald, Earl of Kildare, and other prominent Anglo-Irishmen, with an army of thirty thousand.

Moreover, Barbour (and Haverty, who simply decreases the number and changes the leaders) would have us believe that the great force baulked at attacking Bruce when it came within sight of him. Barbour contends that the reluctance to come to blows was the result of an unintentional stratagem of Robert's. A washerwoman, or in the less prosaic language of the time, lavender woman – from lavandière – went suddenly into the labour of childbirth and, fearful of being left behind and falling into enemy hands, cried out hysterically, attracting Robert's attention. The king ordered an immediate halt and a tent was prepared for the woman until she was fit enough to travel, for, says Barbour,

> This was a full gret curtesy,
> That swilk a King, and sa mychty,
> Gert hys men dwell in this maner,
> Bot for a pour lavender . . .

Perhaps the man who had stabbed a rival to death in church might take pity on a distressed washerwoman, despite the

138

necessity of regaining Carrickfergus as quickly as possible. Perhaps the 'pour lavender' really did exist, although one is bound to question whether washerwomen did form part of military expeditions, particularly of this type, in the fourteenth century during anything other than a full-scale war. There is no evidence to suppose that the toilet habits of the galoglas, or their masters, was any more refined than those of soldiers of later centuries.

Barbour does not relate how long the woman was in labour, but he maintains that the halt convinced the pursuers that reinforcements for Bruce were at hand, and that retreat was the better part of valour. The woman, presumed for the sake of argument to exist, may have been a camp follower. Would her labour pains have halted an army?

Looking at the episode without the trappings of 'gret curtesy', from where, suddenly, did those forty thousand men come? If, as Barbour alleges, they were available in April, why could they not have been raised at the beginning of February? That no army was put into the field as soon as the Scots marched south is evidence that their movements were unexpected or unknown, which explains why Richard de Burgh was caught off his guard at Ratoath. Equally, the government had been taken unawares by events in and around Dublin; had they an army of the size claimed by Barbour they would have faced Bruce quickly and with confidence.

By the beginning of May,[14] Robert Bruce was crossing the sea to Scotland for another attempt to evict the English from Berwick. For him, the Irish adventure was over, and although, doubtless, Edward was vociferous in setting out his achievements and ambitions, he was to receive no more aid from his brother.

Another reason for Robert returning to Scotland was the

139

obvious one that there was no profit to be found in a desert, and a desert is what much of Ulster, Ireland generally, had become. 'There was a great scarcity of victuals in and throughout the realm of Ireland this year' is the laconic remark in the *Annals of Clonmacnoise*, while a later writer summed up the situation succinctly when he termed it the beginning of the 'pestilential period of the fourteenth century'. It was, 'both in duration and intensity . . . remarkably calamitous'.[15] Starting during the Bruce campaign, it lasted 'almost without interruption for eighty-five years. It commenced . . . at a time when the country was labouring under the double scourge of famine and partial civil war, and its effects were to increase the one and render the other general.' Epidemics of epizootics among animals were followed by smallpox among humans, 'then dearth again, with unusual severity of the seasons and intense frosts, accompanied by the first appearance of influenza, and an outbreak of the Barking Mania . . .'

The pestilence caused by the Scots living off the countryside was followed by the depredations of a new band of marauders in that luckless stretch of country between Dublin and the elastic borders of Edward Bruce's dominions in Ulster. After the Bruces departed from Castleknock, a contingent of de Burgh's followers, said to number two thousand, arrived in Dublin, seeking their leader's release. However, Roger Mortimer was also in the city by this time and he was instructed by the government party, who were not convinced that de Burgh should be allowed his liberty, to request the opinion of the English king, hinting strongly that if Edward ordered the earl's release de Burgh must be sent to England. Thus the legislators and administrators, whose efforts had been so often disturbed by the earl, hoped to remove him from the political scene which he had dominated for nearly half a century. But they wanted the decision to rest with the king, so absolving themselves from blame and, they hoped, preventing reprisals from de Burgh's followers, on the one hand, and from the Dublin citizens, who wanted him to stand trial for treason, on the other.

That Richard de Burgh was an old man – he had succeeded his father in 1271 – did not convince his gaolers of his harmlessness. He was still a man of influence and wealth, and his confinement must have been an increasing embarrassment to the government. The 'commonalty of Dublin', who had risked so much in arresting him and placing the city in a state of siege, were not prepared to surrender him so easily, and Edward II, facing problems with powerful barons on his side of St George's Channel, found himself unwillingly responsible for de Burgh's fate.

In the event, the king offered what should have been a compromise acceptable to administrators and citizens. He said that the earl should be sent to England, and that no reprisals were to be taken against Robert Nottingham and his companions for arresting him or, as we have seen, for acting when the government faltered. To placate de Burgh's supporters, the council gave them the king's banner of commission to fight against Edward Bruce, in effect legalising their leaderless anarchy. Communities hardly recovered from the southwards or return marches of the Scots were now visited by this new band who used the king's banner as an excuse to pillage anything that the Scots had overlooked.

Richard de Burgh was released from Dublin Castle in May, following a council meeting held by Mortimer at Kilmainham; but the Dubliners, unconvinced that now he was free the earl would disappear to England, continued to demand that he be arraigned. Mortimer placed de Burgh on bail, to stand trial on 24th June, but before such a sensational event could take place pardons arrived from London, for the justiciar to use at his discretion.[16] Mortimer had no intention of listening to the dictates of the 'commonalty of Dublin' indefinitely, and pardoned the earl, giving him his liberty. Dublin recognised the danger of making an enemy of Mortimer and contented itself with the satisfaction that prompt action in defending its citizens against the Bruces had been appreciated in England. By the end of the year, Robert Nottingham had been called to London to advise the king on Irish conditions,[17] an honour which healed bruised pride and made Dublin believe that England was interested in its opinions.

How far de Burgh had been involved with Robert Bruce's expedition is impossible to assess. He had suffered a disastrous reverse at Connor in 1315, and the arrival in Ireland of Roger Mortimer posed new dangers as the justiciar was determined to be the king's representative in fact, as well as in name. In many respects de Burgh was a product of a past age, more in keeping with the days of Norman freebooters and with his own ancestors who had won land by the sword without risk of interference from officialdom – and certainly without risk of arrest by Dublin merchants. De Burgh himself had won a principality in the manner of the native princes to whom he was so nearly related, and one can imagine that his very 'Irishness' grated with the bureaucrats who distrusted him. Despite the defeat at Connor, he was far more a king than Edward Bruce, whose coronation he doubtless viewed with disdain, and when he died, aged and apparently in retirement, in 1326, the annalists paid him tribute as 'Richard de Burgh, Earl of Ulster, unique choice of the Foreigners and Gaidhil of Ireland'.[18] No such accolade was to be accorded Edward Bruce, who called himself king.

The setback at Connor, however, surely tempted de Burgh

to negotiate, at least with his son-in-law, and even with Edward Bruce, who had caused him to be 'without force or power' after the battle. As he had intrigued with the rivals for the throne of Connacht, so he must have considered using one or other of the Bruces to regain his old prestige. One writer at least[19] suspected him of links with the brothers and offers his arrest as the reason for Robert Bruce deciding not to press his attack on Dublin. Certainly, the retreat from Ratoath could have been a ploy, to be completed when the earl opened the gates of the city, although it lacks conviction as a theory. The earl was aware of the inability of the government to act swiftly, and so if he was in league, secretly, with Robert why did he not simply join forces with him? By retreating to Dublin he put himself at the mercy of the citizens, with whom he was unpopular, with unfortunate results. In any case, his ambitions had always lain in the west and the north, never in the eastern regions of Ireland. He was a chieftain, not a merchant, and it is impossible to imagine one who had led the martial affairs of Connacht presiding over the affairs of commercial Dublin.

Defeat by Edward Bruce, arrest by the mayor of Dublin and even the rivalry of Roger Mortimer did not, individually or collectively, break de Burgh. Nor did it prevent the succession of his young and resolute grandson, William 'Donn', or the Brown Earl as he was known, to the estates recovered in Connacht and Ulster after Edward Bruce's death.

Having returned north, Edward held court at Carrickfergus. For now he was content to rule a subdued Ulster, but kingship must always have a semblance of security about it, and Edward was not secure. He appears as vainglorious, which may once have been a kingly attribute, and with complete disregard for the well-being of his subjects, an attitude which has usually resulted in the death of kings. The failure of his brother to take Dublin must have been a bitter disappointment to Edward, although he surely realised that a famine-racked land could not support an investing army indefinitely. His plan must have been to re-arm and refurbish his troops in Ulster and wait for the south to recover a degree of its prosperity before starting out on his own again.

News from England provided small comfort for the Irish chieftains who still supported Bruce. Early in 1317 two papal nuncios, Cardinal Lucca di Fieschi and Cardinal Guacelin d'Euse, had arrived in England, apparently to negotiate a reconciliation between Edward II and Robert Bruce. They brought confirmation of the excommunication of Robert and any other enemies of the English king who might be invading Ireland or England, and also of the pope's suggestion, made the previous year, that the king undertake urgent reforms in Ireland.

The nuncios' mission did not represent a sudden decision by John XXII to remind the various warring parties of their obligations under the Second Commandment; had that been so, Thomas of Lancaster and his followers would also have been likely candidates for excommunication. Rather, John was seeking to regain some form of power in England, an opportunity having arisen in the king's eagerness to go on crusade, an understandable desire in view of the turmoil at home. Syria, the last stronghold of the Christians in the Middle East, had fallen to the Egyptian sultans in 1291, and while it is doubtful that Edward II sought to recast himself in the mould of his father or his great-grand-uncle, the Lionheart, one can sympathise with his frustration at the ceaseless strife in his islands and understand what caused him to look overseas, where there was but one enemy, easily identified.

The pope cannot have believed that his address to Edward as 'our most dear son in Christ', or his declaration in the Bulls brought by the nuncios that, before he could venture on crusade, the king should have peace at home, would have any effect on Edward's enemies and warring subjects. However, if Edward did turn crusader and leave England for a time, it might be possible to treat with the barons and re-assert the papal influence rejected by Edward I.

John made two mistakes. One was assuming that the English barons would show respect to papal envoys; the other was his refusal to recognise, or at least address, Robert Bruce as King of Scotland. Having seen the English king and received a safe conduct from him, the nuncios set out for Scotland in August. Nine miles from Durham they were attacked and robbed by a local magnate, Sir Gilbert de Middleton. Stripped naked, they were allowed to proceed on foot to Durham, where their fury, in the form of the now meaningless sentence of excommunication, was let loose upon their assailant's head.

Their second error was discovered when, about the beginning of September, they crossed the border and were taken to King Robert at Roxburgh Castle.[20] Although the audience was conducted with every courtesy, Robert refused to open the letter addressed by the pope to the man, 'late Earl of Carrick', *impraesentiarum regnum Scotiae gubernantem*, 'now governing the realm of Scotland'.

Excommunication may have meant little to English barons, or indeed to the Bruces, already sponsored by the church in Scotland; but it lay heavily on the shoulders of the princes of Ulster. The remonstrance sent to the pope had produced no benefit or real solace for them, and pleas that they were not disloyal to the king of England, because they had never sworn fealty to him, were similarly ignored by

John.[21] Their 'loyalty' to Edward Bruce had been a mistake: could it yet be rectified? For the moment, Bruce was all-powerful in Ulster, and, while it cannot be doubted that Domhnall Ui Néill and the other princes who had supported his pretensions had done so for their own ends, they found it more difficult than anticipated to ignore him, or to treat him with the disdain shown to so many high kings in the past. The overlordship of England was replaced, at least in Ulster, with the overlordship of a Bruce.

The famine, noted by all the annalists, outlasted the year, preventing Edward Bruce from marching southwards, although this in no way alleviated the miseries of the people spared his presence. Then, in late March or early April 1318, came news that was to encourage Edward to make a renewed attempt at extending his kingdom. Berwick, the last stronghold of English power in Scotland, fell to Robert. Probably by the treachery of a Berwick burgess, Peter de Spalding,[22] probably by unwillingness to prolong suffering, compounded by hunger inside the town and news of fresh Scottish victories in northern England, the walls were scaled. Edward II, rather unfairly, vented his anger against the mayor and burgesses of the town. They had, he declared, undertaken to defend Berwick for a year from June 1317 and had received six thousand marks to do so. In return for their 'carelessness', he ordered the confiscation of their goods and chattels and the imprisonment of any of their number who had escaped to England. That the invading Scots had plundered and raided at will after gaining the town prevented the king from carrying out the first act of retribution; even so, it can have been small consolation to the unhappy burgesses to learn that the treacherous Peter de Spalding had been executed by Robert Bruce, supposedly for plotting against his life.

By the beginning of June, Edward of England, abandoning
ideas of a Syrian crusade, moved to reverse the humiliation
he was suffering at Scottish hands. For once he was in a
strong position, for the loss of Berwick had exhumed what
little remained of English national pride, so long buried
beneath internecine strife. Bruce had followed up his victory
by burning Northallerton, Knaresborough and Borough-
bridge and extracting a ransom of one thousand pounds
from the inhabitants of Ripon, who, gallantly, had held out
for three days in the besieged Minster church. 'All this
served to discredit [Thomas of] Lancaster, who could no
longer cast the blame for everything that went wrong on the
king', as one historian has pointed out,[23] for both lords and
commons began, albeit belatedly, to see that internal chaos
was leaving the country wide open to aggression from Scotland. How ironic that the same situation had not been recognised and remedied by the princes of Ireland two
centuries earlier.

Reynolds, Archbishop of Canterbury, and the more
moderate barons, notably Aylmer de Valence, Earl of Pembroke, a nephew of King Henry III, came together to attempt
to enforce order and prepare England to eradicate the bitter
memory of Bannockburn. In Ireland, too, a prelate was
found to fill the post of justiciar: Thomas Bickenor, Archbishop of Dublin, whose appointment served to heal the
breach between officialdom and commonalty.

Edward II summoned his army to meet him at York
on 26th July. In Ireland, Edward Bruce, inspired by his
brother's success at Berwick, decided to renew his campaign
in the south. No doubt he imagined that the best of
the English forces would be drafted to York; but his
impetuosity, and a desire to show Robert that he could
more than equal the capture of Berwick, as well as months

of inactivity, combined to send him to the last battle of his life.

'Schyr Edward,' wrote that incorrigible romantic, Archdeacon Barbour, 'was now weill set in gud way to conquer the land halyly; for he had upon his party the Irschery and Ullyster . . .' But he had not all the Irish, nor all Ulster. Earlier that year, Roger Mortimer had moved against the duplicity of the de Lacys: meeting with a refusal to his summons to Dublin, he laid waste their country. Many of the family were slain, including John de Lacy, pressed to death at Trim on Mortimer's orders. *'Seductores et felones Domini Regis'* they were proclaimed, and although several de Lacys escaped to Carrickfergus, they could no longer sway the balance of a contest in the way they had done at Kells, although they were to fight with Edward Bruce in the final battle.

His policy of fire and sword the previous year ensured that Edward could depend on no help south of the border, while many of the lesser magnates, native and English, stood aloof, realising that the administration on both sides of the Channel appeared to be in a semblance of order. Domhnall Ui Néill, and other Ulster princes, counselled prudence, and were ignored. Edward Bruce's 'outrageous surquedry', as Barbour termed his self-assurance, was sufficient counsel for the King of Ireland.

CHAPTER SEVEN

The Battle of Faughart

A great defeat was inflicted in Eile, by O'Cerbhaill, on the foreigners, where Adam Mares was slain, and many other Foreigners along with him. A great army was assembled by Maelruanaidh Mac Diarmada, king of Magh Luirg, and the noblest who were in this army were Toirdhelbhach O'Conchobhair, king of Connacht, and Ualgharg O'Ruiarc, king of Breifne, and Conchobhar O'Cellaigh, king of Ui-Maine, and Tomaltach Mac Donnchaidh, lord of Tir-Oilella. And they proceeded to attack Cathal, son of Domhnall O'Conchobhar . . . And Cathal offered them liberal terms, on condition that they would not go to him, but they did not accept them from him. And these nobles advanced to the very middle of his fortress; but this occurred not through flight or timidity on his part. And Cathal advanced furiously, bravely, against them from out of the houses, and they encountered each other . . .

Thus, through the words of the chroniclers of Loch Cé, we see the state of affairs in Ireland at the beginning of the year 1318. There is a laconic feeling about the passage, as if the anonymous writer wearied of his duty in setting down the history of his island, unchanged as it was from year to year where the bloody disputes of kings and princes were concerned. Certainly, the opening of the new year did not offer hope of peace.

149

Roger Mortimer had made a treaty with Cathal O'Conchobhar in the spring of 1317, in effect recognising him as rightful King of Connacht,[1] despite the fact that he was not even of the *rioghdhamhna*, or blood royal, and could produce no kings among his ancestors for at least six generations, usually a bar to accession. The death of young King Feidlimidh, two years before, the temporary waning of the power of Richard de Burgh, and the generally distressed state of Connacht had enabled Cathal to prepare plans for the advancement of his own branch of the dynasty.

The gradual, perhaps inevitable, disintegration of the old law of tanistry and the emergence of direct descendants of Cathal Crovderg, the king who had died, a monk, in 1224, as rulers of Connacht, to the exclusion of other branches of the O'Conchobhar, may well have been in line with the development of monarchy in England and much of continental Europe. It did not, however, find favour with men who saw their own chance of kingship diminish rapidly. The tradition, established long before the time of St Patrick, that the *rioghdhamhna* constituted the descendants, in the male line, of a common great-grandfather, extending to second cousins and no further,[2] would have excluded Cathal O'Conchobhar, the monopolising influence of Cathal Crovderg's family notwithstanding. The usurping Aedh Breifnach and his brother, Ruaidhridhe, who had already challenged the hereditary, rather than tanistric, principle, were at least more closely related to young Feidlimidh than was the new king. But Cathal had the support, albeit tacit, of Roger Mortimer, whose commission to 'admit the Irish to the full use of English law'[3] gave him an opportunity not only to secure a co-operative ruler in native Connacht but to reduce more the power of the de Burghs.

Toirdhealbhach, the reigning king of the house of Cathal

Crovderg, was no match for the new Cathal. The 'furious and brave' advance resulted in the deaths of those whom the annalists termed a multitude of *nobiles et ignobiles*, among them Brian, son of King Toirdhealbhach, described as 'heir to the sovereignty of Connacht',[4] an indication perhaps that the system of primogeniture was in force. Cathal next 'attacked Connacht . . . and committed great depredations . . . and he assumed himself the sovereignty', deposing Toirdhealbhach, who fled for protection to 'William Burke and all the foreigners of Connacht'. Burke was of course William de Burgh, brother of the Red Earl, whose army had defeated and slain King Feidlimidh in 1316. That Feidlimidh had been Toirdhealbhach's brother shows how far dynastic feeling had altered since the day, in 976, on which Brian Boru had avenged the murder of his brother, Mathghamhain, ruler of Munster.[5]

At the same time, however, it must be said that the family feeling of the ruling house of the Dal gCais seemed never to be emulated by the other royal families of Ireland. In the tenth century, too, the political scene among the kingdoms of Ireland was far less complicated than four centuries later. War was waged against the Danes of Limerick, the Norse of Dublin and local neighbours, usually hereditary foes. By the fourteenth century the picture had become confused: the Land Leapers had departed or long since assimilated with the native Irish; but the factions had increased to include not only rival dynasties and traditionally feuding *tuatha*, but half-Irish magnates such as de Burgh (and many smaller fry), the English administration and, currently, Edward Bruce. We cannot be surprised that Toirdhealbhach, and others, when out of power looked for succour from whichever faction appeared most beneficial. Fraternal feelings were submerged in the struggle for personal authority.

Events in Connacht were, for the time being, of little interest to the English or to Edward Bruce. The news that Robert had captured Berwick, followed by the call to arms of Edward II, had turned the attention of Mortimer to England. Handing over his duties to Archbishop Bickenor, he crossed the Channel, 'leaving his debts unpaid'[6] and forgetting his protégé in Connacht. That summer, too, saw a relatively good harvest in southern Ireland, another reason for Edward Bruce's decision to take to the field.

According to one source,[7] the Anglo-Irish landowners had neither tilled nor sown the greater portion of their lands since the Scots arrived at Olderfleet; neither did they permit the serfs over whom they ruled, nor the *brughachs*, or farmers, who held under them to till the soil. 'They felt convinced that it would be their enemies who would sow seed in their fallows should they prepare them, and that the tenure of the Galls [foreigners] in Ireland was at an end, and on that account resolved to leave nothing behind them for the sustenance of those who were to repossess the country, after their own dispersion.'

One might equally say that there was no point in tilling the soil with the marching and counter-marching of the Scots and other armies, although there is no evidence to support the idea that Richard de Burgh and his fellows regarded their tenure in Ireland as limited. Despite the occasional reverse of fortune, they had no intention of quitting the island as did many of the Dublin merchants when faced by siege. Indeed, the muster raised by Archbishop Bickenor during the course of the year was widely supported; and it must have been this growing opposition, as much as hopes of reaping the results of a good harvest, that led Bruce, in October, to march south towards Dundalk.

The justiciar, we are told, assembled a force 'of all Irland of armit men ... of trappit horse 20,000' and a similar number of infantry.[8] The size, again, can be disputed, although it was sufficient for Edward Bruce's advisers, notably Sir Philip Mowbray and Alan Stewart, to entreat him to wait for reinforcements, presumably from the Irish of Ulster. Yet would they have been forthcoming? Barbour maintains that the chieftains also gave Bruce 'full tendre counsaill', recommending that he defer marching until the 'full accustomed tactics' of the Gael could be brought to bear against the justiciar's army, drawing it into narrow defiles,

> and not to stand in plane melle
> Qhill theta part discomfyt be ...

The threat of excommunication shadowed Domhnall Ui Néill and the other princes of the north; and the return to Scotland of Robert Bruce and the failure of the Dublin expedition were potent reasons for them not to risk their men, or their souls, further. The annalists mention but two native leaders in the final battle: Mac Ruaidhri, King of Inis-Gall, and Mac Domhnaill, King of Airer-Gaeidhel,[9] both of whom were slain; even though one source, usually reliable,[10] gives the opposing army as consisting of only 1,324 men, hardly more than a hasty muster from the northern Pale. Certainly this figure is more realistic than a suddenly materialised twenty thousand, and we can guess with some degree of accuracy that, since the departure of Robert Bruce, Edward's army, which suffered almost as much as the opposition from the years of famine, was about 1,500. The reason for the warning from Mowbray and Stewart may have been doubt as to which side the Ui Néill would support, as well as uncertainty about the chieftains through whose territories Bruce's army had to march.

On 14th October 1318, the feast day of St Calixtus or

Calestis,[11] Edward's forces arrived at Faughart, near where, two years earlier, he had been proclaimed King of Ireland. It was also the anniversary of the Battle of Senlac, or Hastings, at which another foreign invader had gained a throne. The coincidence is too obvious for Edward to have overlooked it, or to have forgotten that his own ancestor had arrived in England with William of Normandy.

Was it presumption that led Edward to do battle at Faughart, or was it fate, one of those coincidences of history? Knowing what we do of Edward's character, from what can be pieced together over the centuries, the scene of the crowning achievement of his career must have been chosen deliberately for what proved to be the final act in the drama. But did he believe that his crown, his hopes for an Irish kingdom, depended on the forthcoming confrontation? Certainly, with the exception of Dublin, he had been remarkably successful; setbacks had been due to his scorched-earth policy and this, apparently, had now been negated by a good harvest. Another victory, near the place of his coronation, would show the English and, of more importance, the faltering Irish chieftains, that Edward Bruce was no less potent than he had been in 1315. A victory on the anniversary of Senlac would add immeasurably to his stature in Irish eyes.

The command of the English army had been given to John de Bermingham, lord of Tethmoy, a member of the Anglo-Norman family which had acquired estates in Connacht after the massacre of the O'Conchobhar princes on Christmas Day, 1295. Described as a man of 'great courage, stallworthines, practised and apt in warres, wise, of a good condition, sober and circumspect', de Bermingham had nevertheless faced opposition before his appointment. It had been the recommendation of the justiciar, Alexander Bickenor, that had resolved the contention among the officials in Dublin, securing de Bermingham the post.[12]

Though my predecessors did not well like him, by reason of evil dishonest counsellors, more of malice than zeal of justice did inform and impute under my predecessor much inconvenience that of him [de Bermingham] did ensue, or it were by reason that my predecessor could not so easily come by certain of his desired purposes, in case the aforesaid lord John Bermingham had the place of mastery of his ancestors by reason whereof the said lord John Bermingham was put by till now in my time . . . [13]

In other words, the rise of the de Berminghams in the west had been viewed by Dublin with misgivings.

There was a prelate at Faughart. Reginald de Sorse, Archbishop of Armagh, Primate of Ireland and episcopal successor to St Patrick, seems to have mustered a host of his own,[14] 'a great cavalcade', with the promise of certain victory. It was, he declared, incumbent upon the Galls – that is, the English – to recover their 'just rights', because the supreme government of Ireland belonged to them 'by right, because the supreme head of the Church had, long ago, granted them the island, together with the herds, and her fruits, and her people'. It was an interesting excuse, considering the earlier admonition of Pope John that neither Edward II of England, nor his predecessors, had paid the slightest attention to Pope Adrian's Bull.

Bruce's army took up its position on the southern side of the hill of Faughart, and he rode among the troops,[15] encouraging them. 'For 'tis certain, if ye are victorious in this battle, there will not be the full of a host or a company to trouble the Gaels henceforth, for the Galls have been in the lowest depth of weakness and despondency, and this is their last rally . . . for it was by treachery they succeeded in subduing

155

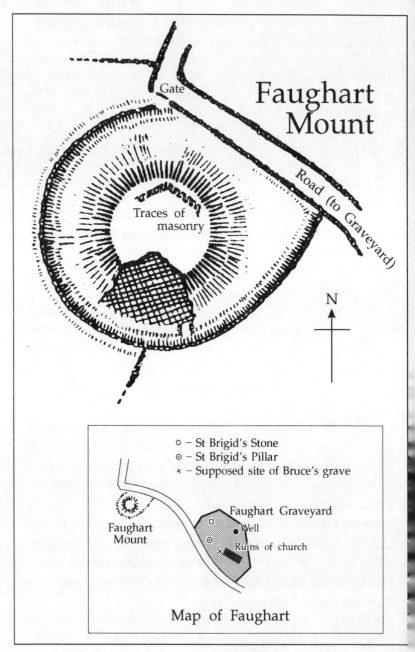

Faughart
Mount

Gate

Road (to Graveyard)

Traces of
masonry

N

o – St Brigid's Stone
⊙ – St Brigid's Pillar
× – Supposed site of Bruce's grave

Faughart Graveyard

Faughart
Mount

Well

Ruins of church

Map of Faughart

the Scots in their own country. But my friends baffle their treachery by displaying superior valour against them . . .'

A stirring speech, if true, although one wonders who took down the words at the time, and certainly one likely to inflame the passions of any Irishman. Whether any Irishman continued to place his hopes in Bruce is another matter. The good harvest might be seen in the customary aetiological sense, but did it signify the approbation of Heaven? Archbishop de Sorse warned the 'Galls' that Bruce must be destroyed before his forces 'tasted of the new fruits of the earth once again';[16] otherwise 'it will not be in the power of England to subdue him . . .' Having previously promised a certain victory over Bruce, the archbishop was wise enough to realise that full stomachs gave additional support to the Scots.

Following the example of Edward I in his Scottish and Welsh campaigns, and, earlier, the precedent of William of Normandy at Senlac, John de Bermingham ordered his archers to send showers of arrows, 'with great resolution' upon Bruce's army. As in Sussex in 1066, the effect was immediate: the Scots fell back from the hillside, leaving many dead or wounded, and, before they could regroup, a cavalry charge, the horsemen 'clad with iron coats of mail from head to foot', drove them into the declivities of the hill. Bruce, remembering Bannockburn and the trouble in which the heavily clad English cavalry found itself, was not to be so easily routed. Rallying his troops, he rushed upon the bowmen, 'whose arrows were then spent', regaining his position and reforming for a 'bloody attack upon the Galls'. Whether the force with which the English horse had thrown itself at the hill prevented it regrouping before Bruce assaulted the bowmen, or whether he fought his way through its ranks, 'slaying three valiant knights with his own hand', is at this distance in time unclear. The very nature of the tract which made up the Irish account of the encounter, the *Battle of Fochart of St Bridget*, is suitably poetic, with actual events sacrificed for dramatic effect. Bruce's career, and his downfall, if fateful for Celtic aspirations, was certainly a fit subject for the heroic, or *Eachtra*, style of the anonymous writer.

There is no evidence that Edward used those vicious calthrops, the steel spikes employed to such devastating effect against the cavalry at Bannockburn. But by stationing his troops on the slopes of Faughart hill did he anticipate a re-enactment of 1314, claiming again the superiority that the New Park had given the Scots? Perhaps he used the schiltron formation to break the ranks of the cavalry, coming upon the archers before they could reload their bows, although recognising the efficiency of the English bowmen generally this seems unlikely. Did the archers find, as did their counterparts at Bannockburn, that the backs of their cavalry obscured the enemy targets once the initial flight had been loosed?

All accounts agree that John de Bermingham and Edward Bruce both displayed great courage. Even Barbour admits that de Bermingham showed considerable bravery and tells us that, on the day before the battle, he disguised himself as a friar, or monk, and entered the Scottish camp, being 'desirous to see Bruce' in order to single him out on the following day and so make a quick end to the battle. Bruce, at Mass, was asked for alms by the visitor, whom he at first ignored. 'The other, being desirous of his desired purpose, never gave over of craving; Bruce looked up and said to those that stood by: "Serve this swase and importunat frier with somewhat, he doeth disturbe me in my servis." "And ever so dooth I meane, unlesse I have my desired purpose," returned the monk.' After Mass was over, Bruce asked for the stranger,

158

'for I swere to you since I saw his face my hart was not in quiet.' He could not be found and Bruce exclaimed, prophetically: 'Well! we shall meete ere; whereas he shall receive a bitter rewarde; but it was evell done for to suffer him to depart, for then wee easily should winne that which great travail is doubtfull to get . . .'

Perhaps John de Bermingham did risk exposure in order to identify his enemy; perhaps, too, Edward Bruce had a premonition of disaster. The story reminds one of King Alfred in the camp of the Danish Guthorm, and certainly legends of prophetic or preternatural visitations before a major battle are common in Irish history, especially if made retrospectively. On the eve of the Battle of Clontarf, three centuries before Faughart, the *leannán sidhe*, or banshee, of the Dal gCais traditionally visited Brian Boru, while a *giolla grádha*, or aide, of the king is said to have seen a phantom army of priests. On the Norse side, superhuman ravens with iron claws and beaks attacked the ships of the Manx pirate, Brodar, whose short-lived claim to fame was the murder of Brian in the aged monarch's hour of victory. Similarly, the *doppelgänger* of Earl Sigurd of the Orkneys, Brian's most distinguished adversary and another victim of Clontarf, had been observed by men in the Orkneys as a forecast of defeat. All such tales added to the romance of war, yet it is possible that de Bermingham did not know Edward Bruce in person, and even more likely that Bruce did not know de Bermingham, who could have visited the enemy camp in disguise.

The death of Bruce is surrounded with equal mystery and romance. An anonymous source[17] maintains that the sortie on the English troops caused a respite in the engagement, enough to allow the Scots to 'take food at the request of the king and noblemen, so that they might be refreshed, to finish the battle with success, rout the Galls to their fortresses, and force them to give hostages and prisoners to secure their peaceable conduct and submission thenceforth . . .' Bruce is said to have left his tent to view the carnage of the morning when a 'shameless idiot', dressed in straw rather than clothing, wandered towards him. The simpleton, 'God's innocent', has long been treated with respect in Ireland, although it is debatable whether convention would have been respected during a lull in battle. However:

[when this] demented person came before the King, he saluted him, and the King returned his salutation in like manner. This demented fellow held in his hand an iron ball to which a long chain was attached, one end of which was tied round his waist, and there displayed many frantic and trifling tricks. When this madman presented himself before the King, he said: 'Oh Gentleman, I am a professor of arts in Ireland, and since I am determined to display my achievements before the King in order to obtain wealth and the honour of knighthood from him, and since I suppose you to be one of the King of Ireland's people, and would be as likely as anybody else to introduce me to the King, I find it necessary to display my feats before you if you wish to view them.' 'I do,' said the King, smiling, 'what feats do you perform?'

'I perform the feats of the iron ball,' said he. 'Well then,' said the King, 'perform your feats for me, and I myself will introduce you to the King.'

The frantic fellow thereupon began to play his uninteresting feats, until finding an opportunity of the King, he gave him a stroke of the ball on the head by which he scattered his brains around. After this act, he ran as fast as he could across the side of the hill, in the direction whence he came . . .

Taken at face value, it is a wholly absurd tale, especially as it has been alleged to be based on Archdeacon Barbour's narrative, while Barbour himself tells us that Edward was killed 'manfullie and verie honourable' by John de Mapas, or de Maupas, 'whose bodie was founde deade lyeing upon the bodie of Bruce'.[18] Barbour would hardly have accepted anything other than an honourable end for his hero, enhanced in this case by the dying king slaying his attacker. The story of the 'fool', however, must not be dismissed entirely; for what cannot be disputed is that several knights on the English side had singled out Bruce early in the conflict, as had Sir Henry de Bohun sought out Robert Bruce before Bannockburn. The rout of the English bowmen may well have made someone turn to desperate measures and, in the disguise of an idiot, enter the enemy encampment. The story of John de Bermingham speaking with Bruce at Mass, and that of the 'professor of arts', have a common source.

Whoever killed Edward Bruce struck off his head and, later, his body was dismembered: that much is known to history. 'The brave defender of Stirling received a mortal wound' at some stage of the fray[19] and the custom of the time demanded some proof that he was dead. While his trunk was almost certainly interred in a rough grave at Faughart, together with slain from both sides, his head was recovered by John de Bermingham and taken either to Dublin or, as one account would have it, to Edward II in London. Even after his death, Bruce's supporters had the final word, however. He had exchanged armour with Gilbert, his harpist,[20] whose head had been struck off and taken to England, they claimed; but it is unlikely that any mistake was made, even allowing for the possibility of a mutilated head. Under English law, the Bruces were traitors and for the head of a traitor there was an ordained place.

The annalists were decisive in their accounts. The *Annals of Loch Cé* recorded:

Edward Bruce, the destroyer of all Erinn in general, both Foreigners and Gaeidhel, was slain by the Foreigners of Erinn, through the power of battle and bravery, at Dun-Dealgan. And Mac Ruaidhri, king of Inis-Gall, and Mac-Domhnaill, king of Airer-Gaeidhel ['king of the island and prince of the Gaels of Scotland', according to Barbour], together with the men of Alba, were slain there along with him; and no better deed for the men of all Erinn was performed since the beginning of the world, since the Formorian race was expelled from Erinn, than this deed; for theft, famine and destruction of men occurred throughout Erinn during his time, for the space of three years and a half; and people used to eat one another, without doubt, throughout Erinn . . .

The simple entry in the *Annals of Ulster*, ever the more sober account, of Edward's arrival – he 'came to Erinn, on the coast of Uladh in the north, with a fleet of three hundred ships' – appears even more tame than usual compared with this vituperative indictment. Even the 'great terrour' noted in the *Annals of Clonmacnoise* pales into insignificance.

'Manifestly, the Gael of Ireland had been by no means generally ready to succumb to and serve the sceptre-sword of the Scottish adventurer,' says Hore,[21] and indeed there was a distinct lack of native chieftains at Faughart. Yet the lament in the anonymous *Battle of Fochart of St Bridget* hardly rings true:

Thus it was that Edward Bruce, King of Ireland, fell, having reigned over the greater part of Ireland [*sic*], over the province of Ulster, the greater portion of Leinster, Munster and part of Connacht two years and two months, and having defeated the Galls and their Irish allies in one and twenty battles, great and small, during three years and five months with great success; and intelligent men think that were it not for the treachery that was acted, it was not in the power of the Galls to defeat him . . .

Intelligent men are wise after the event. The eulogy continues:

Persons worthy of credit who have been intimate with the King, assert that he was an upright pious man, on whose heart the fear of God and the love of man was deeply impressed – that he held injustice and treachery in utmost detestation – that he was a valiant hero, sensible and affable, and friendly towards his subjects, but like an indomitable lion towards his enemies and the doers of injustice – and that he was a learned man well skilled in the various languages of Europe, acquainted with the liberal sciences, but proud of the true royal blood from which he sprung. Woeful, indeed, was the accident that befell the Gaels, the death of the great monarch of Ireland, caused by the deception and treachery of the Galls!

It is a splendid example of partisanship, worthy of the pro-Dalcassian *Cogadh Gaedhel re Gallaibh* and its counterblast, the *Caithréim Ceallacháin Chaisil*,[22] which extolled the Eoghanacht king whose dynasty was eclipsed by the family of Brian Boru. That Edward Bruce should be struck down by 'treachery', rather than in the midst of battle, places him on Brian's level, the king who died at the hands of a fleeing Viking mercenary after the Battle of Clontarf. How woeful indeed! Yet how much more realistic is the bald account in the annals: 'Edward Bruce . . . was slain.' One can almost hear the sigh of relief as the chronicler laid down his pen, having written those words.

The decapitated body of Bruce is said, by his eulogist, to have been carried 'to the house of a gentleman of the family of O'Roddy, who resided on the Hill of Faughart, where a wake and a funeral was held over it, and it was interred with great honours by O'Roddy and his people, in his own family burial ground . . . and they set a coarse unhewn mountain stone over the grave to distinguish it as that of the King of

Ireland . . .' The exact site is today unknown, although an old tradition points it out in the south-western corner of the churchyard of St Monenna, eastward of the mound of Faughart. Of the stone there is no sign.

Once Edward Bruce was dead, the Scots were leaderless. Mowbray had been another casualty and the de Lacys, as so often before, melted away into the autumn mists. There is no reliable account of how many fell at Faughart, but doubtless the survivors made their way to Carrickfergus and thence to Scotland. One account maintains that at Carrickfergus they met reinforcements sent over by King Robert:[23] this is unlikely, for Robert had found the Irish adventure pointless in May of the previous year, although it is possible that, when he heard of his brother's death, he sent ships to rescue what remained of the army. Also, Ulster had not seen the last of the Scots.

'Treachery' on the part of the Galls could apply equally to the King of Scotland, although his desertion of his brother is not surprising. Edward had distracted the attention of England; his death removed that distraction and also a drain on Scottish resources. Had Edward lived, and returned to Scotland, defeated in Ireland, he would have been transformed from a useful distraction into a liability. The impetuous younger brother could be sacrificed.

As if to remove any stain from Robert's treatment of his brother, we have the curious manuscript fragment, 'Robert Bruce's Advice to the Irish'[24] in which, we are told, the king

advised them never to appoint any set battle with the English, nor to jeopard the realme upon the chance of one field; but rather resist and kepe them off from the endangering of the country, by often skirmishing and cutting them off, at straights and places of advantage, to the intent that if the Scotts were discumfeyted they might yet have some power reserved to make new resistance. Again, he forbad them in any wise to make peace, unless by their own turn; for naturally men were dull and slothful by long rest; so that after long peace, through lack of use of arms, men are not able to sustain any great paynes or travail; and therefore he would have the peace but for three or four years at the most.

'Three or four years at the most': the time covered the three and a half years of Edward Bruce's Irish adventure, a period in which any Celtic aspirations to driving the English from their soil were finally destroyed. The adventure proved, more than anything, that the deadly mistrust of Irish chieftains, one towards another, could not be reconciled by what might be termed a third party, in this case Edward Bruce. Hore tells us that the first effect of the Scots' invasion was to elevate the power of the native dynasties of the Ui Néill, 'to reduce which, in Elizabeth's reign, required all the available force in Ireland, backed by frequent armaments from England'. He maintains that the desolate state of eastern Ulster, the result of three years of ravage and famine, allowed the Gaelic clans to reconquer the country, effecting a 'revolution' from English to Irish rule which lasted for three centuries. Certainly, English power, as opposed to that of families such as the de Burghs, waned in Ulster. John de Bermingham, created Earl of Louth for his victory at Faughart, did little more than pursue the stragglers from Bruce's army to Carrickfergus; although it would appear that several of the Scotsmen had, like the Land Leapers of an earlier age, become quickly disenchanted with warfare and were assimilated into the countryside,[25] marrying into native families and bequeathing their surnames, if nothing more, and a vague tradition to their completely Irish descendants. The families of McGotty, otherwise McGorry, and Rogers, both

165

still prolific in Co. Cavan, claim descent from Bruce's followers. At the beginning of the present century, girls of the Rogers family, from Knockbride, Co. Cavan, decided to emigrate to America and presented themselves for the necessary medical examination. The doctor, whom one presumes to have been familiar with Irish characteristics, perplexed them by declaring that they were not Irish. They had, he said, amber-coloured eyes, inherited from the soldiers of Edward Bruce and reappearing after a gap of six hundred years.

Although Edward Bruce never gained authority 'over the greater part of Ireland' requisite for a high king and alleged by his eulogist, his death left a vacuum in which the Ui Néill saw an opportunity to retrieve their ancient power. The Red Earl of Ulster spent his time in prayer at the monastery of Athcassel, in modern-day Co. Tipperary, his fiery soul virtually extinguished, his sword laid aside. The de Lacys and de Verduns were unpunished by the English administration, while, two years after Faughart, the 'people and clergy of Ireland' were readmitted to the doubtful benefits of Magna Carta by Roger Mortimer.[26] English law of life and limb was granted to all Irishmen by edict, and many of the native chieftains found advantage in coming to terms with the superior power. A third of Connacht was granted to Eoghan O'Madden of Ui Maine, 'no English steward to preside over his Gaels, and he and his free clans to be equally noble in blood to his lord De Burgo, contrary to the former decision of these English lords that the Gael was a bondsman while the Saxon was a noble . . .'

Richard de Burgh never regained his former prestige in Ulster, although he may have played a part in driving Domhnall Ui Néill from Tir Eoghan in 1319. If so, it was little more than a token gesture against the part Domhnall had played in bringing Edward Bruce to Ireland. Within a year, Domhnall had returned to his kingdom, which he retained until his death in 1325, a year before de Burgh. Generally, the traditional portrait of internecine strife was repainted throughout the island.

In the late summer of 1326, Edward II of England was forced to abdicate by his wife and her paramour, the erstwhile justiciar, Roger Mortimer. An earlier truce signed between him and Robert Bruce was now regarded as being null and void by the Scottish king, who attacked Norham Castle on the day that the young Edward III was crowned. The attack was beaten off, but in the spring of the following year Robert arrived unexpectedly in Antrim, no doubt taking advantage of the death of his father-in-law, the Red Earl. Sir Henry Mandeville, a kinsman of the defender of Carrickfergus and himself seneschal of Ulster, was forced to sign a truce to last twelve months from 1st August.

But Robert was already a sick man, stricken with what is believed nowadays to have been the first signs of leprosy. Flying columns under Sir James Douglas, Sir Thomas Randolph and the Earl of Mar were sent into England to lay waste to the country as far south as Weardale, and while a significant force raised by Mortimer, including a contingent of over two thousand Flemish cavalry and, for the first time, gunpowder cannon, was defeated by the torrential rain, rather than by the Scots, the time for confrontation between England and Scotland was nearing an end.

In September, Edward II was murdered foully at Berkeley Castle in Gloucestershire, and in the following month negotiations for a permanent truce began. Robert, dying now, demanded complete recognition as King of Scotland and in the spring of 1328 a hundred Scottish knights came south to discuss terms with an English parliament assembled at York.

Edward III, then King of England in name only, ratified the treaty that brought peace:

Since we and some of our predecessors have tried to obtain the rights of rule or lordship over the kingdom of Scotland, on account of which dire dangers of wars have long afflicted the kingdoms of England and Scotland . . . mindful of the slaughters, deaths, misdeeds . . . and innumerable evils which by reason of this kind of wars have happened to both kingdoms, we have conceded, by due common consent and assent of the prelates, magnates, earls and barons and of the commons of our realm in our parliament that the kingdom of Scotland should, within its rightful borders, remain in perpetuity to the magnificent prince, the lord Robert, by the Grace of God, illustrious King of Scots, our most dear friend and ally, and his heirs and successors separately from the kingdom of England, whole, free and quit of any subjection, claim or demand.

The infant son of Robert, the future David II, was engaged to the sister of Edward III and all charters impugning the independence of Scotland were revoked. Virtually four decades after the death of the little Queen Margaret, Maid of Norway, Scotland was recognised by its neighbour as an equal, and the Bruce dynasty appeared secure. The brief restoration of the Balliols, the imprisonment of David II and new wars with England were unsuspected by the majority of Scotsmen, although those close to the throne, who saw the dying king, could hardly expect the transition from seasoned warrior to infant to be easy. Doubtless, many regretted the death of Edward Bruce, and the support given to Edward, son of John, Balliol three years later by a group of dissatisfied Scottish noblemen was hardly unexpected.

In Ireland, in 1329, John de Bermingham, Earl of Louth, was murdered, 'with several of his relatives and followers, to the number of one hundred and sixty or, as others say, two hundred Englishmen being slaughtered by their own countrymen . . .';[27] and four years later the 'Foreigners of Uladh' killed the twenty-one-year-old William, Earl of Ulster, grandson and heir of Richard de Burgh. William was murdered at the instigation of the sister of a kinsman, Lady Mandeville, either in church or on his way to morning prayers in Carrickfergus, but so indignant was the local feeling that when the justiciar arrived to investigate the crime he discovered that a massacre of some three hundred Mandeville supporters had taken place.

The earl's widow, Maud, niece of Thomas of Lancaster, fled to England with her only child, Elizabeth, and a junior branch of the family, fearing that his estates would be transferred elsewhere, seized possession and declared themselves independent of English law. Sir William Burke, who had already Hibernicised his surname, assumed the title of MacWilliam Oughter, or the Upper, while his brother, Edmund, became MacWilliam Eighter, or the Lower MacWilliam. The transformation of the Red Earl's family was complete, and of his direct descendants the sole representative was the little Elizabeth. who, in time, was to marry Lionel, Duke of Clarence, a son of Edward III of England. The ancestress of the house of York, she carried the Ulster title into the English royal family, where it has remained.

Apart from Robert's brief foray into Antrim, no Bruce and no future Scottish king was to concern himself with Irish affairs. By the middle of the fourteenth century, Edward's adventure was consigned to the annals; his attempt to found a dynasty was part of history. Perhaps, after all, he should have fallen in the moment of what was to be his lasting victory, Bannockburn.

NOTES AND SOURCES

CHAPTER ONE. *Insane Counsels, Hopeless Strife*

1. *The Annals of Loch Cé*, edited with a translation by William M. Hennessy, MRIA, when Assistant Deputy Keeper of the Records (London, 1871), and republished by the Stationery Office (Dublin, 1939). They began in 1014 and, according to Professor Eugene O'Curry, MRIA, in *Lectures on the Manuscript Materials of Ancient Irish History* (Dublin, 1861), were continued to 1590 by Brian Mac Dermot of Carrick Mac Dermot, Co. Roscommon. Earlier material could have been lost; what remains is probably based on myriad individual manuscripts.
2. Martin Haverty, in *The History of Ireland, Ancient and Modern* (Dublin, 1867).
3. See *Rome from the Fall of the Western Empire*, by the Revd George Trevor, MA, Canon of York (London, 1868).
4. *Brian Boru, King of Ireland*, by Roger Chatterton-Newman (Dublin, 1983).
5. Guthorm, or Guthrum as he is known in popular histories, was baptised and took the name of Athelstan, being the second of that name to rule East Anglia.
6. The names of the principal kingdoms are today recalled in, but do not correspond exactly to, the present provinces of Ireland.
7. The Norse ancestors of the Normans were ceded the duchy of Normandy by Charles the Simple of France in AD 905.
8. *The Story of England*, by Sir Arthur Bryant (London, 1953).

9. The original appears in the Revd Dr Matthew Kelly's translation of the Revd John Lynch's *Cambrensis Eversus, seu potius Historica Fides in Rebus Hibernicis Giraldo Cambrensi Abrogata,* etc. (Dublin, 1851–2). The story that it was an Anglo-Norman concoction has gained credibility, particularly as the original historian of the invasion was Giraldus Cambrensis, a Cambro-Norman.

10. Haverty, *The History of Ireland, Ancient and Modern.*

11. See 'The emergence of the Ui Néill' in *Ireland before the Vikings,* by Gearóid Mac Niocaill, Lecturer in Medieval History at University College, Galway (Dublin, 1972).

12. *The Annals of Ulster* are perhaps the least biased of the chronicles. Edited by William M. Hennessy, MRIA (Dublin, 1887), they are more correctly entitled the *Annals of Seanadh.* The earliest section of the work, down to 1021, was derived by an eminent cleric, Cathal Maghnuss Mheguidher, from an earlier manuscript, the *Book of Dubhdhaleithe.*

13. See the section devoted to Malcolm II in *Scottish Kings: A Revised Chronology of Scottish History, 1005–1625,* by Sir Archibald Dunbar, Bt (Edinburgh, 1906).

14. She was Hodierna, daughter of Robert de Gernon. De Burgh is said by John O'Donovan, editor of the *Annals of the Four Masters,* to have been, through his mother, Isabel, a natural grandson of Richard I of England. Evidence in favour of the tale is lacking.

15. An account of the Irish system of land tenure may be found in *Gaelic and Gaelicised Ireland in the Middle Ages,* by Kenneth Nichols (Dublin, 1972).

16. Women could, occasionally, inherit land, but only on a 'tenure for life' basis. See Mac Niocaill, *Ireland before the Vikings.*

17. Ibid.

18. *A History of Ireland,* by Edmund Curtis, MA, Litt.D., late Lecky Professor of Modern History in the University of Dublin (London, 1961). See also *Holy Places of Ireland,* by Jim Cantwell (London, no date).

19. Curtis. The *Annals of Ulster* call him 'unique choice of the Foreigners and Gaidhil of Ireland' in his obituary.

20. See Mac Niocaill, *Ireland before the Vikings*.
21. Ibid. 'The inauguration of a king was, symbolically, a mating with the local goddess, with the object of bringing fertility to man and beast in his reign . . .' The symbolism had not been lost completely by the middle ages.

CHAPTER TWO. *Competing for a Crown*

1. According to the ancient Scottish computation, the date of his death was 19th March 1285. On 17th December 1599 James VI of Scotland proclaimed that in and after 1600 the year should begin on 1st January and not, as hitherto, on 25th March, the Feast of the Annunciation. But the proclamation did not introduce what is called New Style, as it did not deduct the ten extra days accumulated erroneously by the Julian method of computing. New Style was introduced in England and Scotland on 14th September 1752. But 1286 is the year of King Alexander's death according to historical computation as it is now reckoned.
2. Quoted by H. E. Marshall in *Scotland's Story* (London, no date, but *c.* 1910).
3. See Mac Niocaill, *Ireland before the Vikings*; also *The Kings and Queens of Scotland*, by Caroline Bingham (London, 1976).
4. From Alba derived the royal honour, Duke of Albany, later transmitted to the English royal family and last held by Charles Edward, Duke of Saxe-Coburg-Gotha (1884–1954), a grandson of Queen Victoria. In common with several other German members of the royal family, he was deprived of his British titles during the 1914–18 War.
5. Bingham, *The Kings and Queens of Scotland*.
6. See *Political Anatomy of Ireland*, by Sir William Petty, Surveyor-General of Ireland (London, 1691).
7. *England before the Norman Conquest*, by Sir Charles Oman, KBE, sometime Chichele Professor of Modern History in the University of Oxford (London, 8th edition, 1938).

8. Chatterton-Newman, *Brian Boru, King of Ireland*.

9. Kent and Essex were worked as sub-kingdoms in the time of Ethelbert of Wessex (d. 858), for example.

10. *Orkneyinga Saga*, edited by Finnbogi Gudmundsson (Islenzk fornrit xxxiv, 1965).

11. Alas, history does not dovetail well enough to suggest that Brusi was ancestor of the Bruces. See 'The Norse predecessors of the Earls of Orkney', by H. Pirie-Gordon, FSA, printed as an essay in London (no date, but *c.* 1920).

12. Ibid.

13. 'A liberal king' is only one of many favourable contemporary comments on Macbeth. See Dunbar, *Scottish Kings: A Revised Chronology of Scottish History, 1005–1625*.

14. *Annals of Tighernach*. The fragment covering the years 974 to 1178 is in a fourteenth-century MS, Rawl. B.488. Much may have been compiled in the monastery of Clonmacnoise, but the authorship of any of the fragments is unknown. See 'The Annals' in *Early Christian Ireland: Introduction to the Sources*, by Kathleen Hughes, Lecturer in the Early History and Culture of the British Isles in the University of Cambridge (London, 1972).

15. Bingham, *The Kings and Queens of Scotland*.

16. Ibid.

17. *British Battlefields: The North*, by Philip Warner (London, 1972).

18. *History of England*, by G. M. Trevelyan (London, 1926).

19. According to *A Short History of Scotland*, by P. Hume Brown, MA, LLD, late Fraser Professor of Ancient (Scottish) History and Palaeography at the University of Edinburgh (Edinburgh and London, 1930), Margaret's father, Christian I, was pressing for the return of the isles to Norway. But, 'as he had not money to pay his daughter's dowry, he gave the Orkney and Shetland Islands instead'.

20. Dunbar, *Scottish Kings: A Revised Chronology of Scottish History, 1005–1625*.

21. *The Age of Chivalry*, by Sir Arthur Bryant (London, 1963).

22. The *lia fáil*, or stone of destiny, is said to have been transferred to

Scotland by early colonists from Dal Riada and thence, by Edward I, to Westminster Abbey. The tale appears in the *History of Ireland*, by the Revd Geoffrey Keating, DD (1570–1650), completed in 1625 and first published in an English translation by Dermod O'Connor in London in 1723. The traditional site of the stone at Tara is today marked by another granite block, which also records the burial place of insurgents killed at Tara in 1798.

23. Bryant, *The Age of Chivalry.*

24. The heir to the throne is 'High Steward of Scotland, Duke of Rothsay, Earl of Carrick, Baron of Renfrew and Lord of the Isles, pursuant to an Act of the Scotch Parliament in 1449', according to *Burke's Peerage.*

25. See note 11 above.

26. *Burke's Peerage* (London, 1865).

27. *Chronica gentis Scotorum*, by John Fordun, edited by W. F. Skene (London, 1871). Fordun, a canon of Aberdeen and perhaps a native of Fordun, Kincardineshire, lived to write four books of the *Scotichronicon*, bringing it down to 1153; but he left collections extending to 1384, when he is said to have died. In 1441 his work was resumed by Walter Bower (1385–1449), abbot of Incholm in the Firth of Forth, who, however, altered and corrupted much of Fordun's narrative. It may have been Bower who changed Marjorie's name to Martha.

28. Edward Bruce was tenth in descent from Malcolm II (1005–34), who married a daughter of Brian Boru.

CHAPTER THREE. *Brothers in Arms*

1. Wherever he was born, 'Bruce was essentially – by upbringing and associations – an Englishman,' declares A. F. Murison in *Famous Scots: King Robert the Bruce* (Edinburgh, 1899). Dunbar, in *Scottish Kings: A Revised Chronology of Scottish History, 1005–1625*, says Robert was born on 11th July 1274, 'it has been supposed at Writtle'.

2. Murison, *Famous Scots: King Robert the Bruce.*
3. *Illustrated Guide to Ancient Monuments*, Vol. VI: *Scotland*, by Professor V. Gordon Childe, D.Litt., D.Sc., FBA, late Professor of Archaeology and Director of the Institute of Archaeology in the University of London, and W. Douglas Simpson, OBE, MA, D.Litt., FSA, Hon.FRIAS, late Librarian, Aberdeen University (Edinburgh, 1954).
4. Bryant, *The Age of Chivalry.*
5. Hume Brown, *A Short History of Scotland.*
6. Murison, *Famous Scots: King Robert the Bruce.*
7. Bryant, *The Age of Chivalry.*
8. Ibid.
9. Robert's first wife, and mother of his daughter, Marjorie, was Isabelle, daughter of Donald, Earl of Mar.
10. Notably C. W. S. Barrow, in *Feudal Britain* (London, 1965).
11. *Edward II: The Pliant King*, by Harold F. Hutchison (London, 1971).
12. See the tale in *Sea Wrack or Long-ago Tales of Rathlin Island*, by Mary Campbell (Ballycastle, 1951). Scott's *Tales of a Grandfather* are, of course, the height of romance.
13. *Family Records of the Bruces and the Cumyns*, by M. E. Cumming Bruce (Edinburgh, 1870).
14. Murison, *Famous Scots: King Robert the Bruce.*
15. See 'Modern Mythology', by Sir Iain Moncreiffe of that Ilk, Bt, in *Books and Bookmen* (April 1972).
16. Cumming Bruce, *Family Records of the Bruces and the Cumyns.*
17. *Annals of Loch Cé.*
18. Cumming Bruce, *Family Records of the Bruces and the Cumyns.*
19. Gaveston was banished to Dublin, as lord deputy. He was married to the king's niece, a daughter of Gilbert de Clare, whose second wife was a sister of the Red Earl. Although Gaveston's Irish career was brief, he appears to have been active in defeating the O'Dempseys of Clanmalier and the O'Byrnes of Wicklow and (according to Haverty) 'opened a road between Castle Kevin

and Glendalough ... and also rebuilt some castles which the Irish had demolished ...'

20. Hume Brown, *A Short History of Scotland.*
21. Bryant, *The Age of Chivalry.*
22. Ibid.
23. The arms of the Drummond family, in whom the earldom of Perth is invested, recall the use of calthrops at Bannockburn, traditionally on the advice of Sir Malcolm Drummond. The armorial supporters stand 'upon a compartment semée of cal-trops'.
24. Hutchison, *Edward II: The Pliant King.*
25. Ibid.
26. *Vita Edwardi Secundi Monachi Cuius dam Malmesbriensis*, edited by N. Denholm-Young (London, 1957).

CHAPTER FOUR. *A Great Fleet-host*

1. John Leland, the antiquary (*c.* 1506–52) became chaplain to Henry VIII, who, in 1533, appointed him 'king's antiquary', with powers to search for records of antiquity in the cathedrals, colleges and religious establishments of England. In six years he collected a 'whole world of things very memorable' and for the rest of his life struggled vainly to arrange his discoveries in some form of order. His chief work was *Commentarii de Scriptoribus Britannicis* (edited by Hall, 1709); but as later historians, among them Camden and Dugdale, 'burrowed' (to use the illuminating expression of the *Dictionary of National Biography*) into Leland's researches, so had he appropriated others' work. In this instance he is quoting Fordun's *Chronica gentis Scotorum.*
2. Despite the traditional view of Richard I – and Bryant, in *The Story of England: Makers of the Realm* (London, 1953), shows that the king was held in esteem by many of his countrymen – he was no asset to England.
3. Of Robert's illegitimate children, Sir Robert died at the Battle of

Dupplin, 12th August 1332; Nigel died at the Battle of Durham, 17th October 1346; Margaret married Robert Glen; Elizabeth married Sir Walter Oliphant of Gask; and Christian was recorded as being in receipt of a pension from her father in 1328 and 1329. Their mothers are unknown.

4. Dunbar, *Scottish Kings: A Revised Chronology of Scottish History, 1005–1625*, quoting the relevant Acts of Parliament.

5. The future David II was born at Dunfermline, 5th March 1323/4. Oaths of fealty were taken to him by the nobility and clergy of Scotland at Cambuskenneth in 1326; and on 17th July 1328 he was married at Berwick to Johanne, sister of Edward III of England. Robert had a younger son by Elisabeth de Burgh, John, who died in childhood and was buried at Restennet Priory, Forfarshire; and two daughters, Matilda, who according to Fordun married 'a certain squire', Thomas Issac, and died at Aberdeen in 1353; and Margaret, wife of William, fifth Earl of Sutherland in 1342/3.

6. Since 1398 the title has been held by the eldest son of the ruler of Scotland. See also note 24, Chapter Two.

7. John Barbour (*c*. 1316–95), Archdeacon of Aberdeen from *c*. 1357 until his death. His epic poem, *The Brus*, was first printed in Edinburgh in 1571 and many times since, including for the Scottish Text Society in 1893–4. Like the Welsh Bishop Asser, biographer of Alfred the Great, Barbour's most redeeming feature was his garrulity.

8. Curtis, *A History of Ireland*.

9. Or was it an apologia on behalf of Ui Néill, against the possibility of Bruce's failure?

10. Curtis, *A History of Ireland*. See also Moncreiffe in 'Modern Mythology'.

11. 'He became putrid while living . . . and died without making a will, without penance, without the Eucharist and without Extreme Unction, as his evil deeds deserved', according to the *Annals of the Four Masters*, compiled from earlier sources five centuries after the king's death. Compare this with the kindly

obituary in the *Book of Leinster*. See *Dermot, King of Leinster and the Foreigners*, by Nicholas Furlong (Tralee, 1973).

12. Curtis, *A History of Ireland*. See also *Edward Bruce's Invasion of Ireland*, by Olive Armstrong, late Helen Blake National History Scholar in the University of Dublin (London, 1923).

13. Alba was the (Irish) Scots' name for the kingdom created by Cineath mac Alpin. See *Scotland's Story*, by Tom Steel (London, 1984). The annalist either confused Edward's ancestry or decided to make it appear more noble than it was.

14. At the same time, while exaggeration was bound to appear in praise of a particular hero, vilification in the case of a tyrant, there is no proof that the annalists, working from early material in most cases, were in any position to decide what was exaggerated. They seem to have regarded their job as writing down what they had heard or had read in older manuscripts.

15. Bryant, *The Age of Chivalry*.

16. Curtis, *A History of Ireland*.

17. Haverty, *The History of Ireland, Ancient and Modern*.

18. *The Holy Roman Empire*, by James Bryce, DCL (London, 1913).

19. See 'The Plundering and Burning of Churches in Ireland, 7th to 16th Century', by A. T. Lucas, MA, D.Litt., MRIA, in *North Munster Studies* (Limerick, 1967).

20. Chatterton-Newman, *Brian Boru, King of Ireland*.

21. Haverty, *The History of Ireland, Ancient and Modern*.

22. 'The Battle of Fochart of St Bridget', by H. Morris, an account of which appeared in the *Journal* of the Co. Louth Archaeological Society, vol. 1, no. 2, July 1905. The account was taken from a manuscript then in the possession of the Very Revd Monsignor O'Laverty, PP, Holywood, Co. Down, transcribed in 1845 by Bryan Geraghty. The origins of the MS are unknown, although the original Irish author had presented events in the *Eachtra* or heroic style, with Edward eulogised in the most partisan manner possible.

23. Murison, *Famous Scots: King Robert the Bruce*.

24. See 'Robert I and the North of England', by Jean Scammell in *The*

English Historical Review, No. CCLXXXVIII, July 1958 (London, 1958).

25. *Calendar of Patent Rolls*, 20.11.1315, 9.5.1317.
26. Armstrong, *Edward Bruce's Invasion of Ireland*.
27. *Annals of Loch Cé*.
28. *Annals of Clonmacnoise*. The translation was made in 1627 by Connall mac Eochagain, who makes no mention of the original authors.
29. 'The Bruces in Ireland', by Herbert F. Hore, in the *Ulster Journal of Archaeology*, vol. 5 (Belfast, 1857), vol. 6 (Belfast, 1858). The account relies much on Barbour, but it is not to be dismissed for that.
30. *Irish Local Names Explained*, by P. W. Joyce, LLD, MRIA (Dublin, 1923). T. J. Barron, the contemporary authority on Brigid, has carried out invaluable research on the saint, particularly in relation to her association with Co. Cavan.
31. *Annals of Clonmacnoise*.
32. Hore, 'The Bruces in Ireland'.
33. Barbour, *The Brus*.
34. *Annals of Clonmacnoise*. Two of his sons are said to have been captured.
35. Armstrong, *Edward Bruce's Invasion of Ireland*.
36. *History of Ireland*, by the Revd E. A. D'Alton, LLD, MRIA (London, 1910).

CHAPTER FIVE. *Edward, King of Ireland*

1. *Annals of Clonmacnoise*.
2. Ibid.
3. *Tanaiste*, from *tanaisteach*, secondary, must not be confused with *comharba*, successor. The designation of an heir beforehand was intended to avoid a struggle on the death of a king. It is now used as the official title of the deputy prime minister of the Irish Republic.

4. See *The Surnames of Ireland,* by Edward MacLysaght, MA, D.Litt., etc. (Dublin, 3rd edition, 1978).

5. Art Ua Ruairc, King of Breifne, had assumed the kingship of Connacht in 1067, after the defeat of Aed Ua Conchobhar. From then until 1102 the throne was the object of a struggle between the two royal houses, the original dynasty being successful in the end.

6. The Dalcassians had gained the upper hand in the eastern portion of what is now Co. Clare on the collapse of the reigning dynasty in southern Connacht, about AD 400.

7. Traditionally, the island was divided into Leath Cuinn (Conn's half) and Leath Mogha (Mogh Nuadhat's half) by Conn Ceadchatach, 'of the Hundred Battles', and his protagonist, Mogh Nuadhat of Munster. There is doubt whether either man ever lived, although Conn's reign has been placed in the first half of the first century AD. The line of division, the Esker Riada, led from approximately the site on which Dublin Castle was later built to the Marey peninsula at the head of Galway Bay. In the tenth century, Brian Boru resurrected the legend when he declared himself ruler of the southern half, Leath Mogha.

8. Curtis, *A History of Ireland.*

9. Sir William Wilde noted in the *Census of Ireland* for 1851 that the 'pestilential period of the fourteenth century was, both in duration and intensity, the most remarkably calamitous in the annals. It dates from 1315 and lasted almost without interruption for 85 years . . .'

10. Armstrong, *Edward Bruce's Invasion of Ireland.*

11. Ibid.

12. Hore, 'The Bruces in Ireland'.

13. Armstrong, *Edward Bruce's Invasion of Ireland.*

14. Hutchison, *Edward II: The Pliant King.*

15. *Calendar of Patent Rolls.*

16. Morris, 'The Battle of Fochart of St Bridget'.

17. See *Louthiana,* by Thomas Wright (London, 1748).

18. *The Tain,* translated from the Irish epic *Tain Bo Cuailnge,* by Thomas Kinsella (London and New York, 1970).

19. The unknown author of the tract on which 'The Battle of Fochart of St Bridget' is supposedly based maintains that he was crowned before the battle.

20. The allegation is made, without substantiation, in Armstrong's *Edward Bruce's Invasion of Ireland.*

21. Ibid.

22. Ibid.

23. Ibid.

24. Dalton, *History of Ireland.*

25. According to Haverty, 'the original Latin of the memorial is preserved by Fordun': see note on p. 279 of *The History of Ireland, Ancient and Modern.*

26. Hore, 'The Bruces in Ireland'.

CHAPTER SIX. *Many Galoglas*

1. *Robert the Bruce, King of Scots,* by Ronald McNair Scott (London, Melbourne, etc., 1982). Scott, who is no less biased than earlier supporters of the Bruces, says that it was a 'considerable army'.

2. *Annals of Ulster.*

3. *Chronicles of England, France and Spain from the latter part of the reign of Edward II to the coronation of Henry IV,* by Sir John Froissart, translated by Thomas Johnes (London, 1842).

4. Armstrong, *Edward Bruce's Invasion of Ireland.*

5. Ibid.

6. Barbour, *The Brus.*

7. *Calendar of Patent Rolls,* 23.4.1317.

8. *Calendar of Ancient Records of Dublin,* by J. T. Gilbert, vol. 1 (Dublin, 1889).

9. *Dublin,* by John Harvey (London, 1949).

10. *Calendar of Patent Rolls,* 20.7.1318.

11. Curtis, *A History of Ireland.*

12. Armstrong, *Edward Bruce's Invasion of Ireland*.

13. Haverty, *The History of Ireland, Ancient and Modern*.

14. Ibid.

15. Wilde, *The Census of Ireland*, 1851.

16. *Calendar of Documents Relating to Ireland*, by J. T. Gilbert (Dublin, 1893).

17. *Calendar of Patent Rolls*, 15.12.1317.

18. *Annals of the Four Masters*.

19. Hore, 'The Bruces in Ireland'.

20. Murison, *Famous Scots: King Robert the Bruce*.

21. Armstrong, *Edward Bruce's Invasion of Ireland*.

22. Fordun gives 28th March for the fall of Berwick; the *Lanercost Chronicles* (translated by Sir Herbert Maxwell, Bt, 1913) say 2nd April.

23. Bryant, *The Age of Chivalry*.

CHAPTER SEVEN. *The Battle of Faughart*

1. Curtis, *A History of Ireland*.

2. *Ireland before the Normans*, by Donncha Ó Corráin (Dublin, 1972). The tradition was supported by Professor Eoin MacNeill in *Celtic Ireland* (Dublin, 1921).

3. Curtis, *A History of Ireland*.

4. *Annals of Loch Cé*.

5. Chatterton-Newman, *Brian Boru, King of Ireland*.

6. Haverty, *The History of Ireland, Ancient and Modern*.

7. Morris, 'The Battle of Fochart of St Bridget'.

8. Hore, 'The Bruces in Ireland'.

9. MacCarthy's translation of the *Annals of Ulster* (Dublin, 1893) identifies these places as the Hebrides and Argyll respectively.

10. The manuscript *Book of Howth* gives Bruce's force as 3,000, although it does not enumerate the opposing side.

11. St Calixtus, pope from 218 to 222, was originally a slave, accord-

ing to Hippolytus, becoming a priest under Zephyrinus, whom he succeeded.

12. *Book of Howth.*
13. Ibid.
14. Ibid.
15. Hore, 'The Battle of Fochart of St Bridget'.
16. Ibid.
17. Ibid.
18. The story is confirmed in Gilbert's *Viceroys*; but also see p. 27 of Barbour's *The Brus*.
19. Murison, *Famous Scots: King Robert the Bruce.*
20. Ibid.
21. Hore, 'The Bruces in Ireland'.
22. In 1905 Alexander Bugge, Professor in the University of Christiania (now Oslo), published a tract of this title, based on the imperfect text in the *Book of Lismore* and on other MSS.
23. Hore, 'The Battle of Fochart of St Bridget'.
24. Ibid.
25. The tradition was widespread in Co. Cavan in the 1980s.
26. Curtis, *A History of Ireland.*
27. Haverty, *The History of Ireland, Ancient and Modern.*

INDEX

INDEX